Seminar Proceedings
Equity Securities Analysis and Evaluation

March 1–3, 1993
Tokyo, Japan

John L. Dorian
Frederick L. Muller, CFA

Andrew Rudd
Gary G. Schlarbaum, CFA
Donald L. Tuttle, CFA, *Moderator*

Sponsored by the

**Association for
Investment Management
and Research**

and the

**Security Analysts
Association of Japan**

To obtain an AIMR Publications Catalog or to order additional copies of this publication, turn to page 96 or contact:

AIMR Publications Sales Department
P.O. Box 7947
Charlottesville, VA 22906
U.S.A.
Telephone: 804/980-3647
Fax: 804/977-0350

The Association for Investment Management and Research comprises the Institute of Chartered Financial Analysts and the Financial Analysts Federation.

ISBN 1-879087-29-4

Printed in the United States of America

12/5/93

Table of Contents

Foreword

This proceedings is a significant "first" for AIMR: Although the seminar on which it is based is the fourth in a series sponsored jointly by the Security Analysts Association of Japan (SAAJ) and AIMR, this volume marks the first time the proceedings is being published in English as well as in Japanese. AIMR is delighted to bring this work to the attention of our broad membership.

Equity Securities Analysis and Evaluation attempts to inform investment professionals worldwide about the essence of analyzing and evaluating equity securities. Using a host of real-life examples drawn from the world of the practitioner, the publication presents some of the main themes of the Chartered Financial Analyst (CFA) candidate program and AIMR's continuing education program for CFAs and non-CFAs. The aim of the proceedings is thus to provide a basic understanding of the issues that equity securities analysts must address.

According to conference moderator Donald L. Tuttle, CFA, who wrote the overview, "This proceedings provides important insights into the common themes of superior equity securities analysis. It shows how both traditional and quantitative analysis can work well, either independently or taken together. It shows the merits of a wide variety of valuation approaches and information on when individual approaches are appropriate. In general, it lays the basis for the novice analyst—a platform which, with proper augmentation and experience, should lead to useful risk–return projections that portfolio managers need to perform their jobs successfully."

Thanks are due to many individuals who guided the program and helped shepherd the resulting proceedings, but two are especially noteworthy: Gentaro Yura, senior advisor to SAAJ, made significant contributions to the success of the seminar, and James R. Vertin, CFA, was instrumental in ensuring that the proceedings was published in book form.

The speakers contributing to the seminar were: John L. Dorian, First Quadrant Corporation; Frederick L. Muller, CFA, Atlanta Capital Management Company; Andrew Rudd, BARRA; Gary G. Schlarbaum, CFA, Miller, Anderson & Sherrerd; and Donald L. Tuttle, CFA, Association for Investment Management and Research.

Katrina F. Sherrerd, CFA
Senior Vice President
AIMR

Biographies of Speakers

John L. Dorian joined First Quadrant Corporation in April 1990. As managing director, he is responsible for trading, equity portfolio management, and research. Prior to his coming to First Quadrant, Mr. Dorian served as corporate director of equity investments at General Dynamics Corporation and was a senior equity portfolio manager with the State of Florida Retirement System. He received B.S. and M.S. degrees in statistics and an M.B.A. in finance from Florida State University.

Frederick L. Muller, CFA, is president of Atlanta Capital Management Company, where he has primary responsibility for portfolio strategy and for managing the firm. Mr. Muller joined Atlanta Capital as a principal after serving as the senior investment officer with Citizens & Southern National Bank. Previously, he held positions at Drexel Harriman Ripley and at Faulkner Dawkins and Sullivan. He is a member of the board of directors of Hill Samuel Investment Management Group, Ltd., of London, the parent organization of Atlanta Capital. Mr. Muller is a former chairman of the Association for Investment Management and Research and of AIMR's Performance Presentation Standards Implementation Committee. He holds a B.A. from the University of Pennsylvania and an M.B.A. from George Washington University.

Andrew Rudd is chairman of the board of directors and chief executive officer of BARRA. Associated with BARRA since its inception, he previously served as president and chief executive officer of the company. Mr. Rudd has also held a professorship of finance and operations research at Cornell University and is a co-author (with H.K. Clasing) of *Modern Portfolio Theory: The Principles of Invest-ment Management* and (with R.A. Jarrow) of *Option Pricing* (Homewood, Ill.: Dow Jones-Irwin, 1982 and 1983, respectively). Mr. Rudd holds a B.S. in mathematics and physics from Sussex University and an M.Sc. in operations research, an M.B.A. in finance and international business, and a Ph.D. in finance and operations research from the University of California at Berkeley.

Gary G. Schlarbaum, CFA, is a partner at Miller, Anderson & Sherrerd and co-director of quantitative research/portfolio management. He formerly served as vice president of the Asset Allocation Division of First Chicago Investment Advisors. Mr. Schlarbaum has also served as a professor at the Krannert Graduate School of Management, Purdue University. He has been an associate editor of the *Journal of Financial and Quantitative Analysis* and of *Financial Review.* Mr. Schlarbaum holds a B.A. from Coe College and a Ph.D. from the University of Pennsylvania.

Donald L. Tuttle, CFA, is senior vice president of AIMR, where he is responsible for member education programs. He previously taught in and chaired the Finance Department at Indiana University. He has also served as professor of finance at the University of North Carolina and as visiting professor at the European Institute of Business Administration, the University of Florida, Georgetown University, and the University of Virginia. He is the author of 22 articles in leading finance journals and 5 books on security analysis and portfolio management. Mr. Tuttle received his B.S., B.A., and M.B.A. degrees from the University of Florida and his Ph.D. from the University of North Carolina at Chapel Hill.

Equity Securities Analysis and Evaluation: An Overview

Donald L. Tuttle, CFA
Senior Vice President
Association for Investment Management and Research

For many years, academicians in the United States and elsewhere believed that equity analysis did not add much value. The presentations from this seminar include such topics as the capital asset pricing model (CAPM), the efficient market hypothesis, and similar theories that many years ago led academicians and many practitioners to believe active equity analysis was of little value. That picture has changed in large part. Many practitioners still strongly believe that adding value, even with good analysis, is difficult. Nevertheless, active equity analysis and active equity portfolio management now have a place in certain segments of all markets and in many segments of many markets.

Several questions can be asked about active equity analysis. What is the role of traditional equity analysis as opposed to quantitative analysis? Are these two approaches in conflict, or are they complementary? Do they reinforce and support one another? Are they really the same, differing only in perspective and methodology? What are the shortcomings of some of the very powerful quantitative methods being used?

Another issue is whether top-down equity analysis is superior or inferior to bottom-up equity security analysis. Should we look at the overall global economy and financial structure, then at sectors, industries, and individual securities, analyzing every phase from the macro down to the micro level? Or is it better to use a bottom-up approach in which individual equities are selected regardless of the market environment at home or abroad?

What is the role of growth-stock analysis as opposed to value-stock analysis? Is one preferable to the other, or do both have a role in equity analysis? Can they be combined to produce a better way of identifying winners among equity securities? Which valuation models are most relevant, most useful, and most applicable? When are they applicable? What criteria are used in those valuation models? How is a discount rate ideally selected? If financial statement analysis is a valuable part of equity securities analysis, how should it be used?

We often discuss ways to determine expected returns in equity securities analysis, but we do not often explicitly discuss risk. How is expected return best combined with the notion of risk in analyzing equities and forming equity portfolios? All these issues and questions are addressed in this proceedings.

Schlarbaum discusses valuation models and financial statement analysis. To illustrate his points, he uses the Coca-Cola Company, an international growth company based in the United States. He provides a brief overview of the Coca-Cola Company and uses Michael Porter's analytical framework to discuss the competitive environment Coca-Cola faces worldwide. Porter, a professor at Harvard Business School, has written extensively on competitive corporate strategy, and his analytical framework has been used in the CFA study and examination program.

Schlarbaum reviews various valuation models based on the dividend discount model. The investment opportunities model highlights value creation arising from situations in which investment opportunities for companies provide a return on equity in excess of the investor's required rate of return. The H-model allows for situations in which the initial growth rate of dividends over H years (the designated near-term horizon, whether it be 5 or 10 years) is assumed to decline over time at a constant rate to a long-term steady growth rate. This model is especially useful for high-growth-rate situations in which the near-term growth rate estimate is high. Schlarbaum also lists some caveats and shortcomings in valuation models and describes the valuation model his firm uses—the excess return model.

The discount rate is a critical input to almost every type of equity analysis model, and Schlarbaum explains how to choose a discount rate for whichever valuation model is used. He reviews some of the CAPM-based formulations to derive discount rates.

The second part of Schlarbaum's presentation deals with financial statement analysis. He discusses accounting issues and how to analyze financial statements with the prime objective of estimating the future earning power of a company. He focuses on major themes critical to equity analysis, including inventory valuation methods under generally accepted accounting principles. In the United States, companies use either the LIFO or the FIFO method to account for inventories. These methods can have dramatically different effects on earnings. The same is true of depreciation methodologies.

Schlarbaum also discusses how to account for investments in affiliate companies, which is becoming an important part of equity analysis. The accounting method differs depending on the nature of the affiliation—passive minority, active minority, or majority ownership situation. Finally, he discusses various approaches to foreign exchange ac-

counting. Such doctrines as purchasing power parity, interest rate parity, and currency forecasting are of critical importance for many multinational corporations. He then demonstrates how some of these concepts apply to the financial statements of the Coca-Cola Company.

Rudd discusses factor analysis and how to use it to analyze individual equity securities. Rudd defines factor models, explains what they can and cannot do, and reviews some of the various factor models in common use.

Factor models are of two varieties: fundamental, or structural, and statistical. Fundamental models apply as many as 12 indexes across many industries and individual securities in an economy, using variables that are familiar to the average analyst. Statistical models have variables that add certain desirable qualities to the models, but these variables are often not recognized as fundamental variables by traditional security analysts.

Rudd also explains how factor models work and how to analyze their explanatory power. He explains the difference between using the root mean square error and the traditional R^2 method to measure error in fitting models to the data. He weaves into his presentation how factor models are related to valuation models. His presentation provides a good understanding of how to use some of the more sophisticated quantitative models that have been developed during the past several years to analyze equity securities.

Dorian presents a different kind of quantitative analysis. Among the models his firm has developed is a quantitative approach to predicting the performance of investment styles. This model distinguishes between periods, for example, when a value approach works better than a growth approach or when small-capitalization equities are likely to outperform large-capitalization equities. His firm has complemented this model with a discipline for forecasting the effectiveness of individual stock selection models. This system assesses the prospective reward for various investment styles to cue timely shifts between growth orientation and value orientation or between large-cap stocks and small-cap stocks.

Dorian reviews three different types of predictive measures. One type is value measures such as the ratio of price to earnings, the dividend yield, and the ratio of price to book value. These variables consistently produce good results but are usually highly variable over time. Dorian uses style forecasts to determine portfolio weightings at any particular time. These weightings determine whether the portfolio is oriented toward value or growth.

A second type measures trends in consensus expectations and earnings surprises. Several U.S. equity analysis firms use this type of measure. The variables have direct effects on individual security returns that occur regardless of the economic or market environment. A third type measures nonlinear trends in return on equity and the small-firm effect. These measures are useful in discriminating between high- and low-return stocks.

Dorian also discusses what an investment manager does once the models for analyzing securities have been completed. Most managers will use an equity portfolio optimizer to identify an efficient portfolio. One option Dorian discusses is a hedged or market-neutral portfolio.

Muller discusses certain key events in the development of modern equity securities analysis. Muller contends that important ideas come along infrequently and often occur during periods of extreme adversity. Modern equity analysis had its beginning in the 1930s; in the 1950s and 1960s, institutional research in the United States attained some of its most sophisticated levels; the 1970s saw the introduction and application of modern portfolio theory, the CAPM, and the efficient market hypothesis; and in the 1980s, new quantitative techniques for equity analysis were developed. Muller then identifies some of the current and future trends in equity analysis worldwide in the 1990s.

The final presentation is a case study in equity analysis based on Merck & Co., a U.S.-based international pharmaceutical company, reportedly one of the best managed ethical drug producers in the world. The case provides an excellent example of common stock valuation. Merck has well-developed strategic objectives, a revamped organizational structure to meet new opportunities, and a broad research and development structure to develop much-needed and potentially profitable products. Yet because of increased competitive pressures, a changing consumer/patient role in drug selection, and the likelihood of significant price-limiting U.S. regulatory actions, the historical valuation of Merck's common stock was called into question in early 1993. The case offers a vibrant example of a turning point in future expectations—and, therefore, current value—for a high-growth, high-value situation. The case solution provides a discussion of a broad range of critical considerations drug stock analysts were weighing for Merck in early 1993.

This proceedings provides important insights into the common themes of superior equity securities analysis. It shows how both traditional and quantitative analysis can work well, either independently or taken together. It shows the merits of a wide variety of valuation approaches and information on when individual approaches are appropriate. In general, it lays the basis for the novice analyst—a platform that, with proper augmentation and experience, should lead to the kind of useful risk–return projections that portfolio managers need to perform their jobs successfully.

Valuation Models and Financial Statement Analysis

Gary G. Schlarbaum, CFA
Partner
Miller, Anderson & Sherrerd

Many variations on the present value model are now available, including the dividend discount, the constant growth, the investment opportunities, the H, the P/E multiple, and the excess return models. Most require choosing a discount rate, and all require an understanding of a firm's financial statements.

This presentation reviews basic valuation theory and financial statement issues using the Coca-Cola Company as an example. The analysis is divided into four parts: an overview of Coca-Cola, a review of valuation theory and how it might apply to Coca-Cola, a review of financial statement analysis, and a demonstration of how these techniques are used to arrive at an investment decision.

Company Overview

Coca-Cola is a straightforward company with a simple process, simple products, and good distribution. It purchases commodity inputs and uses them to manufacture concentrate and postmix. Concentrate is shipped to bottlers that combine it with other inputs and send the finished product to retail outlets such as supermarkets. Coca-Cola also provides concentrate and postmix directly to restaurant outlets.

Coca-Cola states that it has an unparalleled global delivery system. Its infrastructure is in place, which translates into product availability, which translates into sales. It has more than 650,000 employees, 115,000 vehicles, and 6 million vending machines. It has the capacity to deliver 22 billion cases of Coke a year in more than 185 countries. Each year, it makes a $4 billion investment in marketing, which is targeted at 5 billion consumers worldwide.

Coca-Cola's sales distribution by global region is shown in **Figure 1**. The United States is the company's best market, but Europe, the Pacific, and Canada combined also provide significant sales. The distribution of the company's operating income by region reinforces that this is truly a global company. Only a small part of Coca-Cola's earnings are from the United States. In fact, it earns more money in either Europe or the Pacific than in the United States. This distribution of earnings reveals something about the company's margins in the various parts of the world: Where it sells less and makes more, it must have better margins.

Despite its age (106 years), Coca-Cola has a rapid rate of unit growth. As **Figure 2** shows, the unit (case) growth of Coke averaged between 8 and 10 percent in many areas around the world during

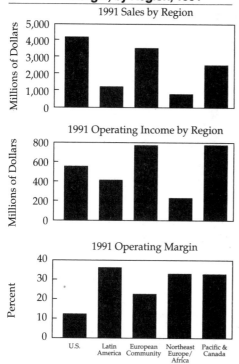

Figure 1. Coca-Cola Sales, Operating Income, and Operating Margin, by Region, 1991

Source: 1991 company annual report.

the past decade. **Figure 3** shows per capita consumption in 24 countries, along with population levels and per capita GNP. In the United States, the average citizen consumes more than 300 8-ounce servings of Coke a year, but the company's penetration is significantly less in some other countries.

Coca-Cola's penetration in Mexico is relatively high despite that country's low level of per capita GNP. Of course, per capita consumption in Mexico could be overstated, because Mexico has a lot of tourism and tourists may prefer Coca-Cola to the Mexican water. Nevertheless, that much penetration in a country where the per capita GNP is so low is encouraging. Many countries with much higher per capita GNPs offer considerable room for additional sales of Coke.

Coca-Cola's great expansion opportunities are an element to consider in evaluating it. Countries such as China and India, which have very large populations and very low penetration, are potentially huge markets for the company. Forty-five percent of the world's population lives in China, India, or Indonesia.

In China, the population exceeds 1 billion, but current per capita consumption of Coke is only eight 8-ounce servings a year. Bringing that per capita consumption up to the level in the United States offers a tremendous growth prospect for the company. China was the first country to sell more than 1 million cases, which it did in the 1930s, before the revolution. Currently, Coca-Cola has $75 million invested in bottling facilities in a concentrate plant in Shanghai.

India has a population of more than 850 million consumers and per capita Coke consumption of three 8-ounce servings a year. In the 1970s, Coca-Cola had a strong presence in India, more than a 60 percent share of the market. The company sold as many as 32 million cases a year before it was forced to leave.

Indonesia has a population of 180 million and per capita consumption of six 8-ounce servings of Coke a year. Indonesia is the ideal soft drink market. About 55 percent of the population is younger than 25. (Young people usually drink more soft drinks than their seniors, and in the United States, as younger consumers become older, they continue to drink a lot of soft drinks.) The average daily temperature in Indonesia is 80 degrees Fahrenheit. Coca-Cola has a 70 percent market share now, and this is another country that has great growth prospects for Coca-Cola.

The soft drink industry has been a business of high returns on equity (ROEs), but how long this characteristic will continue is in question. A useful approach to this question is to use the strategic analysis advanced by Porter.[1]

[1] Michael Porter, *Competitive Advantage: Creating and Sustaining Superior Performance* (New York: MacMillan, 1985).

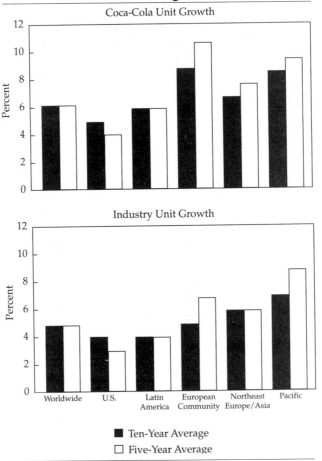

Figure 2. Coca-Cola and Soft Drink Industry Unit Growth in Cases by Global Region: Five- and Ten-Year Averages

Coca-Cola Unit Growth

Industry Unit Growth

■ Ten-Year Average
□ Five-Year Average

Source: 1991 company annual report.

Figure 4 shows how this analysis might apply to Coca-Cola. First, Coca-Cola purchases commodity inputs from worldwide suppliers that are weak in bargaining power relative to Coca-Cola. Little distinguishes one supplier from another other than price. On the other side of the equation are the buyers of Coke—usually, retail outlets. They are small relative to the company and very fragmented. Therefore, and because the bottlers are obligated to purchase concentrate from Coca-Cola, buyers also have little bargaining power with the company.

What about substitutes? The threat of new direct substitutes is relatively low; soft drinks have been around for a long time. One example of a potentially threatening substitute is coffee. There is some concern that young people in the United States are drinking more coffee. If this trend is serious and real, it could be a potential problem for Coca-Cola. Such trends are usually very slow to develop, however.

In the domestic market, Coca-Cola does have some important competitors, such as Pepsi Cola. Pepsi came of age during the hard times of the 1930s. It was a low-price competitor and gained some market share. Pepsi's competition with Coca-Cola in the United States has not translated into effective competition abroad.

What about new entrants? The

Figure 3. Per Capita Consumption of Coke, 1991, and Population and GNP per Capita for Selected Countries, 1990

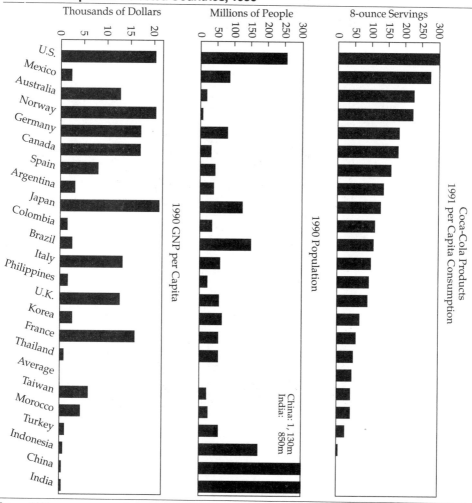

Source: 1991 company annual report.

threat of new entrants is relatively low for Coca-Cola because of barriers to entry in the industry. "Coke" is certainly one of the great brands of all time. People in almost every place in the world know Coca-Cola. In fact, when people ask for a "coke," they are essentially using this particular brand name to mean any cola-type drink. New entrants face some major competition as they try to establish themselves. Coca-Cola and Pepsi have huge retaliatory power and can fight a long fight.

In the United States, private-label brands of some of the retail discount chains could become major competitors. In many cases, the private-label product

is reasonably close in taste. Widespread acceptance of a private-label product would certainly be an important negative for Coca-Cola. Sam's Cola, President's Choice, and other substitutes may be important in the long run, but today, they are no real problem for Coca-Cola.

What about technology risk? The risk of a change in technology is very low, because Coca-Cola has the recipe.

Coca-Cola is a terrific company. For investment analysis, the question is how well that fact is recognized in the marketplace. What is the stock worth? Finding the answer is why valuation models are necessary.

Figure 4.   Competitive Structure of the Soft Drink Industry

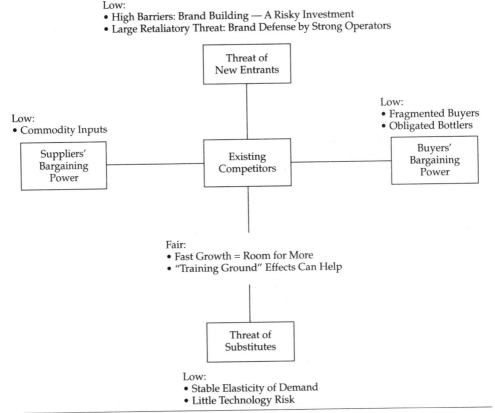

Low:
- High Barriers: Brand Building — A Risky Investment
- Large Retaliatory Threat: Brand Defense by Strong Operators

Threat of New Entrants

Low:
- Commodity Inputs

Suppliers' Bargaining Power

Existing Competitors

Low:
- Fragmented Buyers
- Obligated Bottlers

Buyers' Bargaining Power

Fair:
- Fast Growth = Room for More
- "Training Ground" Effects Can Help

Threat of Substitutes

Low:
- Stable Elasticity of Demand
- Little Technology Risk

Source: Based on Porter, *Competitive Advantage.*

Valuation Theory

To discover what Coca-Cola is really worth and how much the market values the company, several issues must be addressed. First, what cash flows should be discounted back to the present? Second, which one of the many valuation models should be used? Third, what is an appropriate discount rate?

Cash Flows

Analysts discount a variety of cash flows, including earnings, dividends, and free cash flows. Miller, Anderson & Sherrerd uses dividends. Dividends are what matters to shareholders because that is what they receive and what they can spend.

Valuation Models

Valuation is a basic notion with a long history. It was formalized in the United States in 1938 when John Burr Williams wrote his book on the theory of investment value.[2] Williams stated that investment value is the sum of the future cash flows discounted back to the present. This simple notion lies at the heart of any valuation model, no matter how complex. In equation form, the idea is stated as follows:

$$\text{Investment value} = \sum_{t=1}^{n} \frac{CF_t}{(1+k_t)^t},$$

where *CF* is cash flow, *k* is the discount rate, and *t* is the number of periods being used for discounting purposes.

Investment value is the sum of those flows that will occur periodically over time. The value depends on the

[2]*The Theory of Investment Value* (Cambridge, Mass.: Harvard University Press, 1938).

magnitude of the cash flows, the timing of the cash flows, and the discount rates used to discount those flows back to the present. Thus,

$$\text{Price} = \frac{CF_1}{(1+k_1)^1} + \frac{CF_2}{(1+k_2)^2} + \ldots + \frac{CF_n}{(1+k_n)^n}.$$

Several variations on the present value model are the dividend discount model, the constant growth model, the investment opportunities model, the H model, the P/E multiple model, and the excess return model. All of these models are discounted cash flow models, but they use one or more simplifications to make the problem manageable.

■ *Dividend discount model.* In dividend discount models, cash flow is defined as the "dividends" the shareholders receive. Those dividends can be defined specifically as dividends paid or broadly as sales revenue minus expenses minus the annual investment required to generate the revenues. As seen in the following equation, the model discounts dividends for n periods—the number of periods cash flow from the investment is expected to be received:

$$\text{Price} = \frac{\text{Div}_1}{(1+k_1)^1} + \frac{\text{Div}_2}{(1+k_2)^2} + \ldots$$
$$+ \frac{\text{Div}_n}{(1+k_n)^n}.$$

■ *Constant growth model.* The constant growth model is a special case of the dividend discount model. It is a convenient model because it is stated in a very simple form. The key is to accept the assumption that dividends will grow at a constant rate indefinitely:

$$\text{Div}_{t+1} = \text{Div}_t(1 + \text{Growth rate}).$$

This version of the dividend discount model can be simplified into a form in which the security price is equal to the dividend to be paid in the upcoming period divided by the discount rate minus the growth rate, g, which is assumed to persist for a long time—formally, forever. That is,

$$\text{Price} = \frac{\text{Div}_1}{(1+k_1)^1} + \frac{\text{Div}_1(1+g)}{(1+k_2)^2} + \ldots$$
$$+ \frac{\text{Div}_n(1+g)^{n-1}}{(1+k_n)^n}$$
$$= \frac{\text{Div}_1}{(k-g)}.$$

For example, suppose a company will pay a \$5 dividend next period, has a discount rate of 10 percent, and has a constant growth rate of 5 percent. Its stock price should be \$100.

A special case of the constant growth model is one for which the expected constant rate of growth is equal to zero. The price, then, is the ratio of the dividend to the capitalization rate, or

$$\text{Price} = \frac{\text{Div}_1}{k-g} = \frac{\text{Div}_1}{k}.$$

In the no-growth case, the dividends are equal to the economic earnings, which are equal to the free cash flow of the company; therefore,

$$\frac{\text{Economic earnings}_1}{k} = \frac{\text{Free cash flow}}{k}.$$

For example, suppose a company is going to pay out \$10 in dividends and the discount rate is 10 percent. The price, again, should be \$100.

■ *Investment opportunities model.* This model is more complex than the dividend discount models. The investment opportunities model values a company based on the present value of its current earnings plus the present value of its investment opportunities.

Take, as an example, three companies with the characteristics shown in **Table 1**. Many practitioners like to make valuation judgments based on a comparison of P/Es and growth rates or a ratio of the two. Those analysts will like Company C because it is growing faster but has the same P/E as the other companies. This approach is too simplistic, however, in most cases.

Assume the capitalization rate, or discount rate, is 10 percent. Also assume

Table 1. Investment Opportunities Example

Company	P/E	Growth Rate	Dividend
A	10	0.0%	$10.00
B	10	2.5	7.50
C	10	5.0	5.00

Source: Miller, Anderson & Sherrerd.

that each company's ROE is equal to its discount rate. In this case, growth (without external investment) is 1 minus the payout times ROE, and changing the payout will have no impact on the price of the stock:

$$P = \frac{Div}{k-g} = \frac{E(\text{Payout})}{k - (1 - \text{Payout})k} = \frac{E(\text{Payout})}{k(\text{Payout})}.$$

The price for each of the companies would be $100. Company A has a dividend stream equal to its earnings, no growth, and the price is $10 divided by the discount rate of 10 percent, or $100. Company B has a growth rate of 2.5 percent. Dividing its $7.50 dividend by the capitalization rate of 10 percent minus the constant growth rate of 2.5 percent also gives a value of $100. For Company C, dividing $5 by 10 percent minus 5 percent again yields $100 for the price. Reinvesting at the required rate of return provides no value for the stockholder.

If Company C, however, with an earnings base of $10 a share, has opportunities to reinvest half of its earnings each year in projects with ROEs of 15 percent, the total value of the company equals $200:

Year 1:
Opportunity cost (forgone dividend) = $5.00.
Value = ($5.00 × 15%)/10% = $7.50.
Net present value (NPV_1) = $2.50.
Year 2:
Opportunity cost (forgone dividend) = $5.38.
Value = (1.075)($5.00 × 15%)/10% = $8.06.
$NPV_2 = NPV_1 \times (1+ \text{Growth})$ = $2.69.

Putting all of that together results in the additional $100:

$$PV_{\substack{Investment \\ opportunities}} = \frac{NPV_1}{k-g}$$

$$= \frac{\$2.50}{10.0 - 7.5}$$

$$= \$100.00.$$

In short, the stock price will be equal to the present value of the constant earnings stream currently provided plus the present value of the investment opportunities available. Investment opportunities are defined as those opportunities to invest money at a rate of return higher than the required rate of return. It is the sum of those opportunities that make Company C in this situation a more valuable company than the others.

The investment opportunities model is a useful way of approaching equity valuation because it highlights what is important—value creation arising from situations in which investment opportunities provide ROE in excess of required returns.

For Coca-Cola, if this year's earnings, rounded off, will be $2. With a discount rate of 10 percent, that might indicate Coca-Cola stock is worth $20. That would be the value of the constant stream of current earnings. The price of Coca-Cola, however, is about $40, which indicates that the market is paying a lot for Coca-Cola's perceived growth opportunities, such as penetration of markets in Indonesia, China, and India. Investors who do not own Coca-Cola stock believe the market is overpaying for those growth opportunities. They believe the growth rate of Coca-Cola will decline through time.

■ *The H-model.* The H model is useful for analyzing companies for which the rate of growth is expected to decline. It was developed in the early 1980s by Fuller and Hsia.[3] The H-model

[3]Russell J. Fuller and Chi-Cheng Hsia, "A Simplified Common Stock Valuation Model," *Financial Analysts Journal* (September/October 1984):49–56.

identifies an initial growth rate for earnings and dividends (g_i, where i stands for initial period) and contrasts it to a steady long-term growth rate (g_f, where f stands for final period), assuming a company's growth declines linearly. For example, in going from 10 to 5, it goes 10, 9, 8, and so forth. The formula is:

$$\text{Price} = \frac{D_0(1 + g_f) + [D_0(H)](g_i - g_f)}{(k - g_f)}.$$

The left-hand part of the equation is a constant growth model, and the right-hand part captures the value of the above-average growth opportunities that occur in the early years leading up to year H. For example, assuming a $5.00 dividend in Year 1, investment opportunities lasting for 10 years, and that half the total decline occurs by Year 5, then the company is worth $112.50 a year:

$$\text{Price} = \frac{4.76(1 + 5.0) + [5(5)](7.5 - 5.0)}{(10.0 - 5.0)}$$

$$= \$112.50.$$

This value contrasts with the $200 valuation that was calculated in the investment opportunities model, which assumed that the same rate of growth could last for all time.

The analysis of a company's growth prospects is important. The equations will be very sensitive to what is assumed about growth prospects, their magnitude, and their duration.

▦　*P/E multiple model.* The notion underlying the P/E multiple model is that price equals earnings times a P/E multiple.[4] Most analysts derive their earnings forecast from fundamental analysis and estimate P/E multiples from market analysis.

▦　*Excess return model.* The excess return model values companies in terms of their expected returns minus the re-

---

[4]The P/E multiple model and the excess return model are fully described in standard investment texts; see, for example, Z. Bodie, A. Kane, and A. J. Marcus, *Investments* (Homewood, Ill.: Irwin, 1989).

quired return. The difference between the two is a measure of how attractive a security is.

Choosing Discount Rates

A difficult problem posed in almost every one of these models is choosing a discount rate. The three popular ways of estimating discount rates are the capital asset pricing model (CAPM), a multifactor model based on arbitrage pricing theory (APT), and a total risk model.

▦　*Capital asset pricing model.* The CAPM has been around since the 1970s and has been widely used by observers and practitioners of the investment business. The basic formula is

$$K = E(r) = R_f + \beta(R_m - R_f),$$

where

R_f　= risk-free rate,
R_m　= market return, and
β　= sensitivity to market return.

This formula indicates what is really important in determining the ROE and how sensitive the movements of a company's stock price are to the movements of the market as a whole. For Coca-Cola, that sensitivity, often referred to as beta, is probably similar to that of the market or somewhat less. Therefore, Coca-Cola's discount rate should be somewhat less than that of the average company.

The CAPM has been the target of numerous criticisms. Some researchers have found that the security market line—the relationship between returns on securities and their betas—is not as steep as it was initially thought to be.

Another criticism is that how to calculate beta is not obvious. Many different ways have been tried, but at least with individual securities, beta tends to be quite different for different periods. For example, the estimated beta might be 0.7 for the 1975–80 period and 1.25 for the 1980–85 period. Beta has been less of a problem in analyzing portfolios than in analyzing individual stocks.

A third criticism of the CAPM is that

it overlooks what investors are really trying to do. The model is focused on means and variances of probability distributions, but investors are thinking about consumption and how that is spread over time. How those two viewpoints relate to one another is not clear.

The CAPM has also been criticized for considering only one source of risk—market risk. Other systematic influences should also be considered.

Finally, Roll published a well-known critique of the CAPM in 1977 which states that any test of the model is really a joint test of the CAPM and market efficiency.[5]

▦ *Multifactor models.* The criticism that the CAPM focuses on only one source of risk led to the development of the APT model, which states,

$$K = E(r) = \alpha + \beta_1 F_1 + \beta_2 F_2 + \ldots + \beta_n F_n,$$

where F_i is the ith general factor, β is the sensitivity to factor i, and α is the expected return when β is zero. This factor model generates security returns from a series of factors, fundamental or economic, that affect returns. People arrive at the factors in different ways, but the model does allow for more than one systematic source of risk. The model has a certain theoretical appeal and admits no obvious arbitrage opportunities in well-functioning capital markets.

Two APT formulations are as follows:

1. Chen, Roll, and Ross (1986).[6] The factors used in these authors' formulation include real production, inflation, credit premium, and the slope of the term structure. All of them have a certain intuitive appeal.

2. Farrell (1982).[7] Farrell divided stocks into different groups and assigned factors on the basis of those groups of stocks. The groups include growth, cyclical, stable, and energy stocks.

The APT model is not without its problems. Determining the appropriate set of factors is one. Also, the estimation problems are relatively complex, although some analysts have reasonable solutions for those.

▦ *Total risk approach.* This approach is based on the assumption that the discount rate should reflect the total risk of the company—that is, should be the sum of systematic risks, including factor exposures such as interest rates, credit quality, and oil prices, plus unsystematic risk. This approach flies in the face of the theoretical developments of the 1970s.

Choosing a Model

Models seem very precise; when working with them, I often carry the discount rates out to the third decimal place. One can never believe that much precision, however, and more broadly, one cannot always believe the models themselves. Models add clarity and consistency, identify important variables, focus on relationships among the variables, make assumptions explicit, and help to keep the research focused on the important things. Models provide perspective and an understanding of risk. Nevertheless, no matter what model you use and no matter how long you have used it, at the end of the day, you must make the decision. You decided what went into the model, and you must make decisions on the basis of what comes out of the model. Therefore, few practitioners are slaves to their models. The fine balance to maintain is not to ignore the model but not to be a slave to it either.

Financial Statement Analysis

Financial statement analysis is an im-

---

[5]Richard Roll, "A Critique of the Asset Pricing Theory's Tests: Part 1: On Past and Potential Testability of the Theory," *Journal of Financial Economics* (March 1977):129–76.

[6]Nai-Fu Chen, Richard Roll, and Stephen A. Ross, "Economic Forces and the Stock Market," *Journal of Business* (July 1986):383–403.

[7]James L. Farrell, *Guide to Portfolio Management*

portant part of the ongoing work of financial analysts. Sometimes I think it is a lost art in the United States. It is one of those things on which people do not spend enough time. They are more drawn to portfolio theory and do not spend enough time on financial statement analysis.

The basic objective of financial statement analysis is to help understand a company's earning power. Understanding the earning power involves more than financial statement analysis, but the analysis can be very helpful as part of this process.

Accountants distinguish between monetary assets and nonmonetary assets. Monetary assets are those acquired for their exchange value—"quick assets" such as cash, cash equivalents, and receivables. The current values of monetary assets are measured at exchange capacity. Nonmonetary assets are assets acquired for their use value, and they are expected to produce revenues in the future. These assets include inventory, prepaid expenses, and capital assets. They are valued at historical cost, which facilitates income measurement and provides an objective standard. Few companies would want their accountants to assign an estimate of current value to fixed assets each year, and the objectivity criterion permits comparison of financial statements among companies.

Analysts should pay special attention to several areas of financial statements.

Inventory Valuation

Inventory valuation is the first key area to be examined. In inventory valuation, an important choice for many companies as they develop their accounting statements is whether to use LIFO or FIFO accounting. This decision is particularly important for manufacturing companies and other inventory-intensive firms. The matching principle requires that companies favor income

statement accuracy over balance sheet accuracy, which produces a bias toward using LIFO.

The choice of LIFO versus FIFO affects measured returns and measured risk. The LIFO system assigns to cost of goods sold (COGS) the cost of the most recently purchased units of inventory. Consequently, in a period of rising prices, the inventory on the books has lower valuation levels than it would under FIFO valuation. In that situation, using LIFO understates profit margins and profits because it boosts COGS, and it understates current assets. It also provides a higher level of efficiency, as measured by inventory turnover. Because LIFO results in a lowered gross margin, it reduces tax payments. In the United States, the Internal Revenue Service requires companies to use the same inventory valuation procedure for financial reporting and for paying taxes.

Because understatement of assets means equity is understated relative to debt, LIFO increases the leverage ratio. LIFO accounting also produces a lower value for liquidity, because current assets are understated relative to current liabilities.

The use of LIFO sometimes has an effect on company behavior. A company selling more units than it purchases for inventory during a given period will have to dip deeper into its LIFO layers, which means reporting lower COGS, which will result in higher tax payments. The company might choose to accelerate its inventory purchases toward the end of the year—thereby adding newer, higher priced inventory—so as to avoid dipping too far into its LIFO layers. In this situation, the firm's operational activity is being driven by its choice of inventory valuation method.

Economic earnings are the wealth increase the firm experiences during a given period. That wealth increase comes from two sources: operating profits and holding gains. Operating profits are the difference between sales and replacement costs; holding gains are the difference between replacement costs and acquisition costs. Holding gains may be realized or unrealized. Unrealized holding gains are the appreciation on inventory that a firm still holds. Unrealized inventory holding gains are not included in gross margins, so they present an incomplete picture of the company's earnings.

The problems introduced by the use of LIFO and the incomplete picture painted by gross margins are not important in a world with a 2–3 percent rate of inflation. In situations with higher levels of inflation, however, these problems can be very important, because high rates of inflation increase the difference between economic earnings and reported earnings.

Investments

The second key area to consider is investments in other companies. There are three categories of intercorporate investment: passive minority, which is defined as less than 20 percent ownership; active minority, which is defined as 20–50 percent ownership or tangible influence; and majority, which is defined as more than 50 percent ownership.

Table 2 summarizes accounting treatments for intercorporate investments. Passive minority investments are accounted for by using the lower of cost or market (LCM) method. Both income on the income statement and cash on the cash flow statement are equal to dividends. Valuation adjustments are made against shareholders' equity.

Active minority investments are accounted for using the equity method. In this case, the investing company is assumed to have some influence over the operations of the subsidiary company. This situation calls for a different accounting method because, if the company has influence on the subsidiary, it can drive earnings by influencing the dividend policy of the subsidiary. Rather than having that flexibility, management is required to use the equity method, which is essentially one-line consolidation. The fractional share of earnings is included as income of unconsolidated affiliates on the income statement, and an investment account equal to the acquisition cost is shown on the balance sheet. This account is adjusted upward each year for income earned at the subsidiary level. A company using this method reports dividends only as cash flow.

Table 2. Summary of Accounting for Intercorporate Investments

Accounting Method	Balance Sheet	Income Statement	Cash Flow Statement
LCM (< 20 percent ownership)	Investment account = LCM Valuation adjustment: Made vs. share equity (not income)	Dividends = Income	Dividends = Cash
Equity (20–50 percent ownership)	Investment account = Acquisition cost Basis increases with income, decreases with dividends	Equity in income in unconsolidated affiliates	Income – Undistributed income = Dividend = Cash
Consolidation (> 50 percent ownership)	Investment account eliminated Assets and liabilities added Minority interest (share equity)	Revenues and expenditures added Minority interest in net income subtracted	Cash from consolidating Minority interest in income = Noncash expense

Source: Miller, Anderson & Sherrerd.

If a company has a majority interest in and exercises control over a subsidiary, the two companies' accounts are consolidated and the investment account is eliminated. The assets and liabilities of the subsidiary are added to the balance sheet of the parent, and the revenues and expenses are added to the income statement.

This exercise was designed to provide a basic understanding of the nature of the firm's earnings and the factors that influence them so that analysts will include this kind of analysis in their valuation process. For example, in valuing Coca-Cola, intercorporate accounting is important because about $2 billion of Coca-Cola's $10 billion in book assets represent active minority investments in bottlers around the world.

Accounting for Foreign Operations

Accounting for foreign operations is another important area of financial statement analysis. U.S. firms must use U.S. generally accepted accounting principles, not foreign practices, for their foreign operations. These firms' accounts are governed by Statement of Financial Accounting Standards (SFAS) No. 52, which deals with foreign currency translation.

The objective of SFAS No. 52 is to clarify the effect of changes in foreign exchange rates on income. The translation has three basic elements: (1) At the end of each period, assets and liabilities are translated at the exchange rates then in effect; (2) revenues, expenses, and net income are translated at the average rates in effect during the accounting period; (3) a translation adjustment is made to shareholders' equity to balance the accounts.

The implications are that income figures will vary with changes in exchange rates. Income will not be affected by balance sheet translation, because shareholders' equity absorbs the balance sheet translation. Think of bal-

ance sheet exposure in terms of the net investment. To the extent the company is able to borrow and fund the investment in the foreign country, it will be able to reduce its investment and foreign exchange risk exposure. Declines in the value of the assets will be offset by declines in the value of the liabilities. Analysts forecasting earnings for global companies should try to anticipate the effects of currency translation.

The Investment Decision

To pull together the various concepts discussed in this presentation, I will illustrate how Miller, Anderson & Sherrerd (MAS) values Coca-Cola. The analysis date is January 6, 1993, and June 30, 1995, is the investment horizon.

MAS uses the excess return model to identify potential investments. The process involves estimating expected return, taking dividends into account, for a three-year period and estimating the price at the end of the third year, which is determined by using the P/E multiple model.

The first step in the process is to determine forecast earnings. **Table 3** shows company earnings per share (EPS), growth, and P/E estimates for 1990 through 1995. Coca-Cola has been a very reliable growth company, and we expect that pattern to continue. The growth rates MAS is projecting continue to be about 19 percent for the next three years. The assumptions from which the earnings estimates were derived are reasonable; for example, MAS assumed that Coca-Cola's growth rates will con-

Table 3. Earnings, Growth, and P/E Estimates: Coca-Cola, 1990–95

Year	EPS	Growth	P/E
1990	$1.02		
1991	1.21	19%	34.2
1992	1.43	18	28.9
1993	1.68	17	24.6
1994	2.00	19	20.7
1995	2.39	20	17.3

Source: Miller, Anderson & Sherrerd.

tinue at about the same pace as in the previous 5–10 years.

Table 4 shows the specific variable estimates used for Coca-Cola in the MAS excess return model. We use two earnings estimates—a high and a low—because of the difficulty of predicting the earnings of any company. For Coca-Cola, the spread between the high and the low is relatively narrow. The high–low range would be much wider for, say, Ford Motor Company, for which 1995 earnings are harder to forecast.

The discount rate is 10 percent, which might be considered conservative because long-term rates in the United States are about 7 percent. We argue, however, that a discount rate similar to that of the Treasury bond is appropriate for Coca-Cola because of its historical performance when times were really difficult. We have done a lot of analysis of the behavior of Coca-Cola—its earnings, stock price, and so forth—between 1928 and 1938, the period of the Great Depression in the United States. What

Table 4. Variable Estimates for Excess Return Model: Coca-Cola

1995 projected low EPS	$2.30
1995 projected high EPS	2.60
Post-1995 growth rate	15.00%
Post-1995 payout rate	40.00%
Discount rate	10.00%
Relative P/E assumption	1.70
Beta	1.10
Modifier inputs	
Earnings momentum	5
Earnings surprise	6
Price momentum	7
Conceptual appeal	2
Estimated annual dividend	$0.56

Source: Miller, Anderson & Sherrerd.

people wanted then were long-term bonds. When the price level is going down, a long bond is a great thing, unless it defaults, and U.S. government bonds do not default. Coca-Cola grew every year during the Depression with the exceptions of 1932 and 1938, when earnings growth was only slightly negative. Coca-Cola did not outperform T-bonds each year, but it did in many of the years, as shown in **Figure 5**. If you

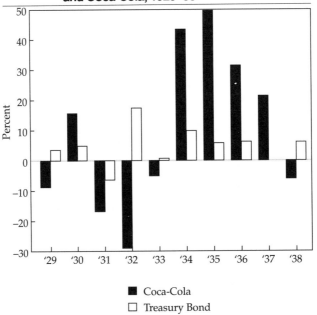

Figure 5. Total Returns of Long-Term Treasury Bonds and Coca-Cola, 1929–38

■ Coca-Cola
□ Treasury Bond

Source: Miller, Anderson & Sherrerd.

Note: Coca-Cola return estimated as increase in average price; dividends ignored.

owned Coca-Cola during this 10-year period, each $1.00 invested became $3.23; if you owned T-bonds, it became $1.54. Given that type of performance, a discount rate for Coca-Cola that is not too far from that of T-bonds is reasonable.

The relative P/E is assumed to be 1.7, which is somewhat high. The relative P/E is used in conjunction with our assumed P/E ratio for the market to derive the anticipated stock price in 1995, which is then discounted at 10 percent.

Figure 6 shows annual high and low P/Es for Coca-Cola from 1927 to 1991. The company's P/E valuations were very high during much of the 1930s, so the high P/E multiple assigned to the company in Table 4 is not at all unreasonable.

MAS will adjust expected returns for various potential market effects, identified as modifier inputs in Table 4. Companies with earnings momentum and conceptual appeal, for example, will have their excess returns adjusted upward.

A summary of our analysis for Coca-Cola is shown in **Table 5**. From 1991 to 1995, the low EPS growth rate is 17 percent and the high is 21 percent. The implied post-1995 ROE is 25 percent. To introduce some variation into the relative P/E multiple, we examine 1.53 and

Figure 6. Annual P/E Ranges: Coca-Cola, 1927–91

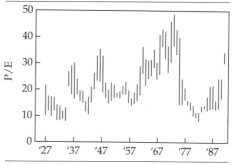

Source: Miller, Anderson & Sherrerd.

Note: Prices = annual high and low prices; earnings = actual earnings.

1.87 as possible high and low relative P/E multiples rather than focusing only on 1.70. That approach gives us a low absolute multiple of 23.3 and a high of 28.4 based on the P/E for the market in 1995. The dividend yield is 1.4 percent.

This summary translates, using a total of one modifier, into the low, high, mean, and modified price projections presented in **Table 6**. The table also presents the total returns to the prices and the excess of each price over the required rate of return. Against our required rate of return of 10.0 percent, the mean price of $64, for example, gives an excess return of 10.4 percent. In this framework, Coca-Cola is an attractive stock.

Table 5. Summary of Excess Return Model Analysis: Coca-Cola

Low EPS growth rate 1991–95	17.0%
High EPS growth rate 1991–95	21.0%
Implied post-1995 ROE	25.0%
Low relative P/E multiple	1.53
High relative P/E multiple	1.87
Low absolute P/E multiple	23.3
High absolute P/E multiple	28.4
Modifiers	
Earnings momentum	0
Earnings surprise	0
Price momentum	0
Conceptual appeal	1
Total modifiers	1
Dividend yield	1.4%

Source: Miller, Anderson & Sherrerd.

Table 6. Excess Return Model Estimates: Coca-Cola

Price projections	
Low price	$53.00
High price	74.00
Mean price	64.00
Modified price	66.00
Total return to:	
Low price	12.30%
High price	27.70
Mean price	20.40
Modified price	22.10
Discount rate	10.00
Excess return	
Low price	2.30%
High price	17.70
Mean price	10.40
Modified price	12.10

Source: Miller, Anderson & Sherrerd.

Question and Answer Session

Gary G. Schlarbaum, CFA

Question: Ford Motor's earnings are difficult to estimate because the range of possible future earnings is wider than Coca-Cola's, which is a defensive growth company. Can excess returns for Ford and Coca-Cola be made comparable by increasing or decreasing discount rates?

Schlarbaum: One of the real purposes of our models is to compare excess returns across companies. At MAS, different analysts follow different companies, and we use the model to communicate with one another. We deal not only with the differences in the kinds of companies but also with differences in the people doing the analyses. Some insist on being conservative, others try to be objective, and still others try to push the stocks they follow all the time. Those differences must be taken into account in using the numbers the analysts produce. If the same person is analyzing both Ford and Coca-Cola, the numbers might be more comparable, but you must understand what approach the analyst is using. Is the analyst using normalized or peak earnings? Where does he or she think we are in the cycle in the particular year in which the analysis is being done?

Our research reports and portfolios at the end of a day have a high degree of congruity. The stocks that have the highest excess returns tend to be the best represented in the portfolios, and with higher weights. The issue we wrestle with constantly is how best to adjust our estimates.

Question: In the excess return model, absolute value is used to evaluate a potential investment. Because estimating the discount rate is so difficult, should relative figures be used instead of alphas in picking individual stocks?

Schlarbaum: Every stock you analyze might have an excess return greater than 10 percent. If that is the case, you may have a problem with your analysis, because if every stock looks attractive, something is amiss. We do rank all the stocks we analyze according to excess return. Although every return listed is an absolute number, we base our decisions on the relative ranking of those numbers.

Question: In your presentation, you discussed Coca-Cola's performance only in the 1930s. Can the model be used to estimate Coca-Cola's current price?

Schlarbaum: The example I provided was an attempt to determine what kind of return to expect, given the current price, during the next three years. The conclusion is that the expected return for Coca-Cola for that period is about 20 percent. Compared with the 10 percent that we believe is right for the level of risk of Coca-Cola, the investment appears to be very attractive.

If you conclude that Coca-Cola is not an attractive investment, you have a different assessment of the company's prospects. Perhaps you think that the market believes this company will grow at 5 percent a year rather than 15 percent or that the company does not have wonderful investment opportunities or that earnings will grow less than we estimated during the next three years or that the relative P/E is too high. The model simply takes a set of inputs we consider important and tells us what we can expect.

Factor Analysis Approach to Analyzing Individual Securities

Andrew Rudd
Chairman and Chief Executive Officer
BARRA

Factor models decompose returns on assets into a set of basic elements and describe the exposure of the assets to those factors. Because these models use data efficiently and effectively, a growing number of investment managers are applying factor models in risk management, portfolio optimization, and valuation.

Factor analysis is a useful tool for analyzing individual securities and portfolios of securities. This presentation describes what a factor model is, provides examples of various types of factor models, and discusses the explanatory power of factors. It will also demonstrate some specific applications and review factor models that might be applied to asset valuation.

Factor Models

Factor models posit that asset returns can be generated by the returns to a set of common factors and the exposure of the assets to those common factors. The formal definition of a factor model is:

$$R_i(t) = a_i + \sum_{j=1}^{k} X_{ij}(t)f_j(t) + \varepsilon_i(t) ,$$

where

$R_i(t)$ = return on security i in period t,

k = number of common factors,

$X_{ij}(t)$ = exposure of security i to factor j, and

$f_j(t)$ = return on factor j in period t.

The aim of a factor model is to decompose the returns on assets into a set of k primitive factors, which describe the movement of those returns. The security exposures or loadings on those factors describe the type of company involved. The part of the return that cannot be explained by the factors is captured by the error term. This analysis decomposes, or unpacks, the returns on assets into a number of more basic elements and describes the exposure of the assets to the factor returns in terms of factor loadings.

Factor models essentially average the returns for each factor. The averaging process can be used for two important functions. One is to forecast asset returns; the forecasts for the f's, together with the factor loadings, the X's, are used to forecast the asset returns. The second use of factor models is to determine an asset's risk from the variability of the historical factor returns with the factor loadings. Factor models are also a good way to estimate portfolio risk.

One way of estimating risk is to calculate the full covariance matrix. This method is inefficient, however, because it requires a great many historical data, namely, the correlations and variances of each individual asset. To get a reasonably efficient estimate on a universe of 1,000 assets, for example, more than 80 years of monthly data are needed. Obtaining 80 years of monthly data that are representative of current conditions is impossible. The historical data will also not account for the changing nature of the assets, particularly if companies are changing debt ratios, merging, acquiring companies, or so forth. For those 1,000 assets, 500,000 data items must be estimated, each with statistical uncertainty. Thus, calculating the full covariance using historical data is not a meaningful or useful way of estimating risk.

The market model was the first approach to getting around the data problems inherent in risk estimation. The market model is a single-factor model in which the one factor is identified as the market. The risk, or volatility, of a stock has two components:

$$Var(r) = \beta^2 Var(r_m) + Var(r_r) \, ,$$

where

$Var(r)$	=	expected security variance,
β	=	sensitivity to the market risk,
$Var(r_m)$	=	expected market variance, and
$Var(r_r)$	=	residual variance.

A stock's risk, then, is related to the exposure of that stock to the market and to the residual, or nonmarket, risk. The proportion of risk explained by the market is the systematic risk coefficient, beta. The volatility not explained by the market is called the residual risk, or nonmarket risk. For a universe of 1,000 assets, only 1,000 betas and the variability of the market are needed to estimate systematic risk. If, in addition, one estimates the residual risk of each asset (an additional 1,000 numbers), the full risk model is composed of a total of 2,001 data items.

One advantage of the single-factor model over the full covariance matrix is that the data can be used more effec-

tively, which reduces the statistical uncertainty surrounding the estimation of the parameters. Multiple-factor models allow even more precise estimates.

Applications of Factor Models

Factor models have several important uses. The primary applications are in portfolio analysis, optimization, performance attribution and analysis, asset allocation, and asset valuation.

▨ *Portfolio analysis.* Factor model technology permits the estimation of asset risk. That information can then be used to understand the risk of the portfolio, both in absolute terms and relative to a benchmark. Factor models can be used to identify the strategies, the sectors, the industries, and the stocks that contribute the most to portfolio risk. They can also measure the tracking error of a portfolio relative to an index.

▨ *Optimization.* Factor models can be used to construct an optimal portfolio that reflects the analyst's judgments about a set of stocks and their expected returns. To the extent that an analyst does not have judgments, the optimization program effectively produces an index fund.

▨ *Performance attribution and analysis.* Factor models can be used to measure a portfolio's risk–return trade-off over time. A portfolio's return can be attributed to various component strategies, and then the component returns can be analyzed to determine whether the reward was sufficient for the level of risk taken. For example, the risk–return trade-off on a sector bet can be calculated and evaluated.

▨ *Asset allocation.* Risk models can be constructed for whole asset classes or large sectors of asset classes. These models facilitate analysis of asset allocation decisions. Two approaches are commonly used. One, based on the returns of the asset classes, estimates the risk of the allocation from the time-series properties of returns. The other approach takes the fundamental and economic exposures of the asset classes as the inputs and bases the risk of the allocation on the estimated covariance of those exposures.

■ *Asset valuation.* To construct a portfolio, factor models can be used to estimate the sources of value directly or, by using the residuals coming from the factor model, indirectly. On average, the residuals should be normally distributed (i.e., the factor model explains the average return). A large specific return in one period, therefore, may be expected to be unusual and to be followed by a reversal in the next period. In fact, the residuals from factor models exhibit a great deal of negative serial correlation—a large positive return followed by a negative return, and vice versa. Offsetting this negative serial correlation in the residuals is usually some positive serial correlation in the factor returns.

This statistical finding suggests that managers could develop tilt funds to capture the effect of the positive serial correlation. For example, the manager could tilt the portfolio toward value, growth, or foreign exposure to capture the fact that these factors accumulate through time. Alternatively, the manager could structure a hedge portfolio having long and short positions to capture the negative serial correlation from the residuals. This portfolio would go long on those assets that underperformed in the previous period, in the hope of obtaining the positive rebound in the residual, and go short on the stocks that had a positive return in the prior period, in the hope of benefiting from the expected negative residual return.

Types of Factor Models

The two main types of factor models are fundamental and statistical.

Fundamental Models

The fundamental factor model bases the factors on fundamental infor-

mation. The Japanese equity model BARRA developed in collaboration with Nikko Securities will illustrate this type of model. This model has 12 company-specific risk factors (indexes): systematic variability, size, success, growth, financial leverage, value, trading activity, interest rate sensitivity, specific variability, foreign sensitivity, exposure to second-section stocks, and non-Tokyo-stock-exchange exposure. All 12 factors are company-specific characteristics that are available to analysts. The model also contains an industry, or sector, effect. Companies are assigned to 1 of 40 industries.

The model requires that firm-specific returns be uncorrelated and independent of the factor returns. These assumptions lead to a definition of the covariance matrix in terms of a matrix of exposures:

$$V_t = X_t F_t X_t^T + \Omega_t,$$

where

F_t	= factor covariance matrix,
X_t	= matrix of asset exposures, and
Ω_t	= diagonal matrix of specific variances.

The subscript t indicates matrix transposition. This model provides an efficient way to use the data and is a computationally easy way to develop the risk of portfolios.

Fundamental models are useful for explaining and forecasting risk and for constructing portfolios. The factors can be used to identify reasons for past performance. These models facilitate making factor bets and adding new companies to a portfolio, and the models may be adapted for changes in company circumstances such as mergers and acquisitions.

Statistical Models

Statistical factor models derive the factors implicitly by using a statistical approach, either maximum likelihood estimation or factor analysis. The assumptions of a statistical model are more stringent than those of a fundamental model. The assumptions are as follows:

- The asset exposures are constant.
- The specific returns are independent of the factor returns.
- The specific returns are uncorrelated among the assets.
- The factor returns are independent with zero mean and unit variance.

Given these assumptions, the covariance matrix of asset risks is given by

$$V_t = X_t X_t^T + \Omega_t .$$

This type of estimation is complicated and requires several steps. Typically, the estimation is performed on groups of assets rather than one asset at a time. The following steps are required to estimate such a statistical model:

1. Cluster assets into mutually exclusive groups (to avoid singularity problems).

2. Calculate group returns.

3. Perform a maximum likelihood estimation on the grouped asset returns. Maximum likelihood estimation is an iterative process that produces the number of factors, k; the matrix of factor loadings on the asset groups, X_G; and factor returns, f.

4. Compute the matrix of asset ex-

posures, X, by historical time-series regression of excess stock returns against the statistical factor returns.

Statistical models are useful for risk forecasting and portfolio construction, but they are difficult to use for explaining risk and past performance. These models can be used to estimate factor exposures for new stocks. Keeping the asset exposures constant, however, does not allow for changes over time.

Macroeconomic Variables

Many analysts believe that factor models should include macroeconomic variables, and a number of studies have addressed the relationship between macroeconomic variables and stock returns. Macroeconomic variables affect asset returns in several ways, as **Figure 1** illustrates. Relationships are found at

Figure 1. Macroeconomics and Stock Returns

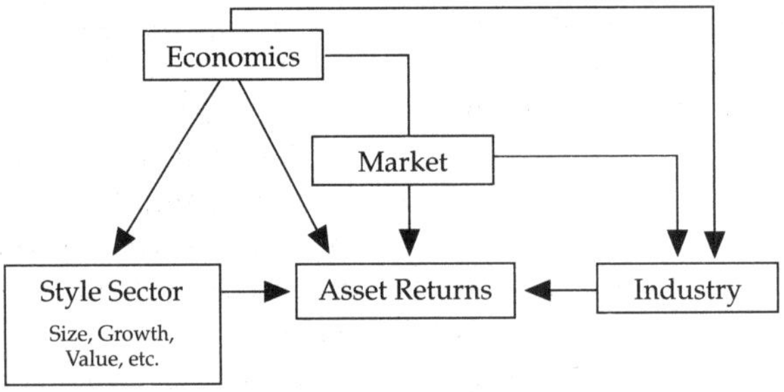

Source: BARRA.

market, industry, and company levels. The economic environment affects the market, which influences the returns on all stocks; affects industries and style in sectors, such as value versus growth, in different ways; and affects individual assets within a given sector or style in different ways. Thus, the macroeconomic environment can affect asset returns through the industry of the asset and perhaps directly through the market.

The question is: Can the effects of macroeconomic variables be attributed to the different sources? For example, do changes in the price of oil have a more important impact on the returns to oil companies than the market return does? Using British Petroleum (BP) as an example, **Table 1** shows the effects of the U.K. market and of oil price changes on BP and on oil and gas industry excess returns. The market explains about 40 percent, compared with about 4 percent for oil prices (in U.S. dollars), of BP's excess return. If BP is excluded from the market, the explanatory power of the market (because BP represents such a large proportion of it) drops only to 35 percent. Oil price changes explain an even smaller portion of the oil and gas industry excess return. Depending on the inclusion of BP, the market explains 40–50 percent of oil industry excess returns; the price of oil itself explains only 3–4 percent. Thus, the price of oil is less important to BP and to the industry than what happens in the marketplace as a whole.

Table 1 also shows the analysis in terms of residual, nonmarket, returns. When the market's effect is removed, the price of oil is very important; it explains about 20 percent of BP's and the industry's excess returns. The price of oil does have an important influence—not on BP's total excess return but on its nonmarket return. This result is also found in other industries. In most cases, one should model the impact of these macroeconomic variables in terms of residual returns rather than the total returns of the stocks themselves.

The connections between macroeconomic variables other than oil prices and asset and sector/style returns tend to be weaker, which is why the factor model does not include economic variables. Other common factors (such as the market) explain stock returns better than macroeconomics. The economic variables do influence the market, but noneconomic events (psychology, political events, and so on) also affect the market as a whole, causing it to be riskier than it would be in their absence. These other factors are more closely related to asset and factor returns than are macroeconomic variables.

Tests of Explanatory Power

Statistical techniques can be used to analyze the explanatory power of both fundamental and statistical models. The R^2 statistic, which measures the portion of variability a model explains, is a convenient statistic. When comparing models, however, particularly across markets or across models with different volatilities, the R^2 can provide a biased result. For example, a 30 percent R^2 in a very risky market will have a different meaning from the same 30 percent in a less risky market, because the volatility bases are different. To make these numbers comparable, the root mean squared error (RMSE), which measures error in fitting each model to cross-section returns, should be used. The RMSE is not as affected by different levels of volatility as R^2.

The tests of the explanatory power of a model must be consistent. Out-of-

Table 1. Market and Price Change Effects on Returns

Return	Market Excess	Market Excess (no BP)	Oil Price Change (£)	Oil Price Change ($)
Excess return				
BP	0.3970	0.3486	0.0469	0.0369
Oil and gas industry	0.5084	0.4727	0.0394	0.0287
Residual return				
BP	0.0146	0.0288	0.1725	0.1906
Oil and gas industry	0.0000	0.0008	0.1986	0.2060

Source: BARRA.

Note: Figures are R^2s from monthly regressions, June 1982–December 1991.

sample tests are appropriate for most applications, although in-sample testing may be relevant for some. Tests comparing results for fundamental and statistical models should use the same number of assets and periods.

Table 2 illustrates the differences in explanatory power between a fundamental and a statistical model of the European market. The in-sample period is January 1985 to December 1989, and the out-of-sample period is January 1990 to December 1991. The test statistic was the RMSE. Typically, an in-sample test provided a better fit with a statistical model and an out-of-sample test provided a better fit with a fundamental model. The reason is that statistical models match themselves to the specific data set and so explain the various characteristics of those data. When moved to the out-of-sample period, the model tends to deteriorate, primarily because the in-sample relationships were period specific and may be wrong when examined over a longer period. In contrast, the fundamental model looks for relationships. Under the assumption that those relationships have some permanence and some forecasting ability through time, the fundamental model is much less likely to be subject to out-of-sample error.

Table 2. The RMSE in Fundamental and Statistical Models: European Example

Model	Minimum	Mean	Maximum
Fundamental model			
In-sample	2.94	5.13	9.26
Out-of-sample	4.02	5.42	7.90
Statistical model			
In-sample	1.90	3.78	5.85
Out-of-sample	5.36	7.21	10.06

Source: BARRA.

In this example, the in-sample mean error is approximately 25 percent lower when the statistical model is used and the out-of-sample mean error is 25 percent lower when the fundamental model is used. These results are essen-tially identical to what one would observe in other regions of the world.

Fundamental factors have the advantage of being interpretable. They are based on fundamental and market-related characteristics commonly used in security analysis. They can be named, and portfolios constructed using them. They are also incisive; they divide the market into well-defined slices. These factors contribute significantly to risk or to persistent or cyclical positive or negative exceptional returns.

Statistical factors are more difficult to interpret than fundamental factors. Additional statistical techniques such as rotating the data or grouping the assets can help modify the factors to make them more meaningful while preserving the model's explanatory power. Rotation, for example, involves statistical transformation of the matrix of factor loadings on groups of assets (or the assets themselves).

Asset Valuation Tools

Factor models are valuable tools for asset valuation. This use focuses on determining pricing relationships, rather than risk, among securities. The factor model approach is entirely consistent with traditional valuation models such as the dividend discount model (DDM).

The basic DDM holds that expected return is the sum of dividend yield plus expected capital appreciation. It is a constant growth model. The formula is

$$E\{r\} = \frac{d}{p} + g \,,$$

where

$E\{r\}$ = expected return,

$\frac{d}{p}$ = dividend yield, and

g = expected capital appreciation.

Rearranging the terms, the formula can be rewritten as

$$p = \frac{d}{E\{r\} - g} \,.$$

An alternative formulation (from the world of bonds) is

$$p = \frac{d_1}{(1+z)} + \frac{d_2}{(1+z)^2} + \ldots + \frac{d_t}{(1+z)^t}.$$

If

$$d_t = (1+g)^{t-1}d,$$

then

$$p = \frac{d}{z-g},$$

where z is $E\{r\}$.

Under the constant-growth assumption, price, earnings, and dividends all grow at the same rate.

How might one use this model? To the extent that the expected return, $E\{r\}$, is equal to the risk-free rate, i_f, plus a fair risk premium, $\beta(\mu_B)$, plus α, the DDM can be rewritten as

$$\alpha = \frac{d}{p} + g - \left[i_f + \beta(\mu_B)\right].$$

This formula says that the alpha on the stock is equal to the dividend yield plus the growth rate, less the risk premium plus the risk-free rate.

A problem with DDMs is that estimates of g are difficult to obtain and usually optimistic. One solution to the problem is to smooth the data. Quantitative managers try to smooth the data by narrowing the applicability of the model, such as by using industry or economic sector, or by using a three-stage DDM model. The typical three-stage DDM model uses a starting growth rate that reflects the analyst's special insight and ends with an equilibrium growth rate. In the interim years, a transition growth rate between the starting and ending rates is used.

The DDM can be used to solve for the rate of return (given the dividend stream, d_t, and the market price, p), or for a fair price, p^* (given a fair rate of return, z^*, and the dividend stream, d_t). In the first method, solving for the rate of return, a stock's alpha equals the difference between the stock's rate of return and the fair rate of return $(z - z^*)$. In the second method, solving for the fair price, a stock's alpha equals the proportional difference between the fair price and the market price $[(p^* - p)/p]$. Although the first method might be the standard way to use DDMs, both methods are in some sense *ad hoc*: There is no theory as to why they should work.

Another approach to asset valuation is to use the DDM in conjunction with accounting relationships. The basic accounting relationship is that book value equals the previous period's book value, b_{t-1}, plus earnings, e_t; less dividends paid, d_t. Then, if an abnormal set of earnings is defined as earnings in excess of some fair rate of return, $e_t^* = e_t - z(b_{t-1})$, with some algebra, price can be defined as beginning book value plus the present value of abnormal earnings:

$$p = b_0 + \frac{e_1^*}{(1+z)} + \frac{e_2^*}{(1+z)^2} + \ldots \frac{e_t^*}{(1+z)^t}.$$

A simple model for the persistence of abnormal earnings is

$$e_{t+1}^* = \delta e_t^* + \text{Noise}_t$$

where

$$0 \leq \delta < 1 + z.$$

This model says the abnormal earnings in the current period are equal to a fraction of the abnormal earnings in the last period plus some noise. To the extent that a company has a surprise in earnings, then, this surprise will attenuate through time.

A little more algebra produces the following model:

$$p = c_1 b_0 + c_2 e_0 + c_3 d_0,$$

where

$$c_1 = 1 - k = 1 - \left(\frac{z\delta}{1+z-\delta}\right);$$

$$c_2 = \frac{k(1+z)}{z} = \frac{(1+z)\delta}{1+z-\delta};$$

$$c_3 = -k.$$

This version is a linear factor model describing the price of the assets in terms of such characteristics as book value, earnings, or dividends (represented by the X), and the "price" of each characteristic, f; that is,

$$P = Xf + \varepsilon.$$

This approach can be used in a cross-sectional regression to estimate the parameters c_1, c_2, and c_3 across a group of similar companies and determine the alpha on the stock as the difference between the model price and the market price:

$$p_{market} = p_{model} + \text{Error}$$
$$\alpha = \frac{p_{model} - p_{market}}{p_{market}}.$$

Quantitative managers use linear pricing models, in which a factor model is merely set up in price space and the deviations from a set of average prices in the marketplace are described as effectively and efficiently as possible. The manager can then set up a strategy based on the deviations from such a model to determine the relative pricing among assets. Market-neutral and tilt portfolios are examples of strategies that use this approach.

The difficulty in using linear pricing models is in controlling differences among companies. To the extent that the linear pricing model is fitted to a universe of companies that are not homogeneous, the coefficients c_1, c_2, and c_3 are likely to be misestimated. One could handle this problem by using dummy variables, but doing so may cause statistical inefficiencies.

The factor model uses described here are a good starting point to applying more complex and esoteric techniques, such as the application of neural networks and other artificial intelligence approaches, to try to explain the price of assets in terms of other characteristics.

Conclusion

In summary, fundamental and statistical models are useful in risk forecasting and portfolio construction.

Adding intuitive factors can lead to robust models because the manager can deal with them mentally. Intuitive factors allow the use of risk decomposition and performance analysis because the manager can relate the portfolio returns to intuitive characteristics.

Most importantly, factor models are more robust than full asset covariance models. Factor models take the data available and use them in the most efficient and effective way. These models are thus becoming a popular area of research, with widespread application in finance. In particular, their use in risk management, portfolio optimization, and valuation is growing.

Finally, factor models provide a basis for successful investment strategies in relative valuation.

Question and Answer Session

Andrew Rudd

Question: When using the DDM, if the model is not perfect, how can portfolio managers determine whether that discrepancy from the model prediction is alpha or just an error?

Rudd: Factor models are used to try to explain differences in valuation across a universe of stocks with a variety of attributes. The aim is to determine a model price that reflects those different attributes. The difference between the market price and model price is defined as an "error." It is just a difference, however, and the hope is that the difference contains information.

To determine whether that difference contains or does not contain information, BARRA builds a model that captures as many different attributes of stocks as possible and then uses a back-test to test the resulting difference for information. I do not advocate using any of these models without testing for information for a historical period.

In general, the purpose of using models is to distill a whole series of different information sources into something meaningful—to separate the true signal from the noise of random events occurring in the marketplace. Distinguishing between signal and noise requires experience and sensitivity in testing.

Question: Is the return-reversal phenomenon applicable to Japan?

Rudd: The return-reversal phenomenon has been extremely strong in Japan in the past, and it could be used quite effectively in paper portfolios to achieve a significant rate of return. Return-reversal strategies are typically high-turnover strategies. These strategies are great for brokers, because they produce commissions. They are also good for those who have low transaction costs. Otherwise, they are more of academic interest. In the United States, the benefit of the return-reversal phenomenon is not constant; it gets stronger or weaker through time, in cycles. The cause might be related to the number of people using the same type of implementation to capitalize on the return-reversal phenomenon.

Question: Please comment on the appropriate use of macroeconomic variables in factor models.

Rudd: The use of macroeconomic data depends on its timeliness. Macroeconomic data on the price of oil, interest rates, and other characteristics for which there is a market price are timely and can be used. Such data as government-provided quarterly estimates of national product are much less usable. However determined, macroeconomic data are much less useful for risk prediction than many people think. On the other hand, macroeconomic data can be useful for valuation purposes.

Question: What are the possibilities of using artificial intelligence or neural networks in factor models in the future?

Rudd: I am somewhat positive about the uses for artificial intelligence methods, particularly neural networks, in fairly well-defined problems with some nonlinearities for which linear models do not work or could potentially be misleading. For example, a couple of my former students have used neural networks for predicting changes in bond ratings, in which some important nonlinearities appear to be at work.[1] They demonstrated that they can achieve models that are better than simple statistical regression models.

The trouble with neural networks is that we lack knowledge about how to test them and measures of significance. Also, depending on how you set them up, they can be unstable. Applying them is almost an art rather than a science. Investment institutions around the world are trying to do something with these techniques, but to my knowledge, few have yet achieved anything of value in using them.

[1]Soumitra Dutta and Shashi Shekhar, "Bond Rating: A Nonconservative Application of Neural Networks," *Proceedings of the IEEE International Conference on Neural Networks,* July 1988: 443–50.

Macromodels for Identifying High-Performance Market Sectors

John L. Dorian
Managing Director
First Quadrant Corporation

Investment style is the most important determinant of equity returns, but the market goes through phases in which some styles are less rewarding than others. Now, a model has been developed that can help anticipate which style will outperform in any given environment.

A popular practice in the United States is to segregate managers by style—value managers, growth managers, large-capitalization managers, small-capitalization managers, or combinations thereof. This practice has considerable merit, particularly in performance measurement. Investment style shapes the pattern of equity returns more than any other element of the investment process. For example, in a year that rewards value, almost all growth managers will suffer, and vice versa. In 1992, U.S. value managers outperformed growth managers. During the prior six years, except in 1988, growth managers dominated. In the six years from 1980 to 1986, value managers were dominant except in 1982.

Most managers are trapped in their styles. Therefore, they can have long periods of perverse (negative-value-added) returns relative not to their benchmarks but to their markets. Many clients are not sophisticated enough to use the correct benchmark and may terminate an excellent manager who underperforms the S&P 500 for several years when, in reality, the S&P 500 was the wrong measuring stick.

A discipline that anticipates which style will be rewarded is a valuable tool for the selection of both portfolio management and manager. This presentation will describe a model First Quadrant Corporation is developing that will predict which investment style will outperform the others in any given environment.

Quantifying Style

A number of firms have methods for quantifying style. BARRA, for example, has identified 13 common factors. They are called common factors because all stocks, or a portfolio, can be described in terms of exposure to them. The factors are

▦ *Variability in markets.* Risk prediction, analogous to beta and sigma, based on stock price behavior.

▦ *Success.* Past success of the company, as measured by the stock's performance and earnings growth.

▦ *Size.* A size index based on assets and capitalization.

▦ *Trading activity.* An indicator of share turnover.

▦ *Growth orientation.* A predictive

index for earnings-per-share (EPS) growth based on growth in assets and Institutional Broker's Estimate System (IBES) forecasts of earnings growth.

■ *Ratio of earnings to price.* Various measures of EPS divided by market price.

■ *Ratio of book value to price.* Book value of common equity per share divided by market price.

■ *Earnings variation.* Variability of earnings and cash flow.

■ *Financial leverage.* Relationship of debt to equity on the firm's balance sheet.

■ *Foreign income.* Proportion of total income identified as nondomestic in origin.

■ *Labor intensity.* Ratio of labor cost to capital cost.

■ *Dividend yield.* Predicted dividend yield of common stock.

■ *LOCAP.* Dummy variable indicating small capitalization.

The First Quadrant model supplements the BARRA common factors with four proprietary factors:

■ *Earnings revision.* The change in IBES earnings estimates and the earnings surprise.

■ *Residual reversal.* The tendency for stock prices to reverse over the short term.

■ *Relative strength.* The stock's price behavior during the prior 12 months.

■ *Nonlinear trend in return on equity.*

The different sources of style have varying degrees of importance, as **Table 1** shows for linear factors for 1973 through 1990. During this period, the average return on dividend yield, for example, was 6 basis points a month, which means that high-yielding stocks outperformed other stocks that were identical in their exposure on all other factors except yield by 6 basis points a month on average during this 18-year period. Two factors, earnings revision and residual reversal, are of particular interest.

Earnings Revision

The return to earnings revision, which is the monthly change in the mean consensus forecast for a particular company, was 50 basis points. Because earnings surprise is highly correlated with earnings revision, the two were merged. Earnings surprise accounted for about 20 percent of the power of the earnings-revision factor.

This factor is interesting because of

Table 1. Common-Factor Monthly Returns, 1973–90

Factor	Mean	Standard Deviation	t-Statistic
BARRA			
Variability in markets	−0.10	1.43	−1.0
Success	0.24	1.16	3.0
Size	−0.13	0.82	−2.3
Trading activity	−0.08	0.76	−1.5
Growth exposure	0.06	1.14	0.8
Earnings/price	0.29	0.76	5.6
Book/price	0.25	0.73	5.0
Earnings variations	−0.01	0.67	−0.2
Financial leverage	−0.04	0.48	−1.2
Foreign income	−0.03	0.36	−1.2
Labor intensity	0.03	0.59	0.7
Dividend yield	0.06	0.82	1.1
LOCAP	−0.19	1.91	−1.5
Other			
Earnings revision	0.50	0.60	9.9
Residual reversal	−0.52	0.90	−6.9

Source: First Quadrant Corp.

the possibility that it is being arbitraged away. In 1992, using earnings revision, a manager could have had superior performance by buying companies for which the consensus forecast of earnings was disastrous. Those companies outperformed the companies for which improved earnings were forecast. In the early 1980s, this inefficiency was so powerful that positive earnings revisions that occurred in January could still be exploited in June; so the optimal model involved lags of one to five months, with decaying weight as time passed. By the late 1980s, three-, four-, and five-month lags had no value; one-month-old information had marginal value. In 1992, the factor was perverse, so the approach did not work at all. This factor will not necessarily be perverse from now on, but this inefficiency will no longer have the same power as in the past because more people are now aware of it and are exploiting it.

This consensus information was available only on a monthly basis until fall 1991, when it went to a weekly tape; it became available on a daily tape in fall 1992, and now, it is available on a real-time basis. This inefficiency is a prime example of what terrifies quants—that something they are exploiting or that has worked historically will no longer work. They should incorporate some feedback loop in their models to stop them from continuing some strategy even after it stops working. Earnings revision is still a very powerful inefficiency, but to exploit it, you must do it rapidly.

Residual Reversal

The return to residual reversal, which measures the tendency of stock prices to reverse over the short term, was –52 basis points. Residual reversal is far more powerful in Japan than in the United States, because transaction costs are so much higher in Japan. These inefficiencies must be analyzed both statistically and practically to determine whether they are exploitable—that is, whether any gain will be left after paying the transaction costs.

Only brokers can afford to build a stand-alone strategy around residual reversal, but that does not mean managers should ignore it. On the margin, it has value. Once a decision to trade has already been made, managers and traders can use residual reversal to enhance implementation. Short-fuse alphas, very-high-turnover strategies, should be used this way.

Residual reversal can be calculated many ways. After a model has explained as much of the raw return as it can, what remains is the residual, which is referred to as company-specific factors or an error term. If this residual has been large in one direction or the other, the evidence is overwhelming that it will reverse direction during the next short holding period. Some analysts measure residual reversal over one month, but First Quadrant's work indicates that the bulk of the residual reversal occurs during the next five days, and half of the power of that bulk is concentrated in the first day.

The best way to calculate the residual reversal is to take each residual each day and orthogonize it so it is unrelated to the prior day's residual. Multiple regression can be used to find the optimal weightings for each day.

The Evolution of Quantitative Models

The United States is in the midst of an evolution in quantitative portfolio management methodologies. The first-generation approach sought to predict returns based on the average historical reward to a univariate model. Generation I managers would identify an attribute such as yield, rank all their stocks by that attribute, and buy the most attractive ones. The models were unsophisticated, univariate models, but given a long enough horizon, they worked. Consider low-P/E tilts, for example. With a long horizon, a manager need not do much more than buy the lowest P/E stocks. Rarely, however, will a client tolerate five or six years of perverse returns waiting for the long run. Analysts used Generation I models many years ago, and they were never referred to as quants.

Quants came into their own in the 1970s with multivariate models (Generation II). Quants would identify several inefficiencies and tilt toward all of them (mostly through a naive equal-weighting tilt, but some through regression)—identifying what they thought the optimal weighting should be on these tilts. This approach had the distinct advantage of dampening the volatility of a manager's alpha; instead of five or six years of underperformance, it would last only two or three years. In the United States, however, two or three years is a long time; frequently, the investment horizon is a quarter.

The innovation in the third-generation approach was to apply an optimizer to the second-generation model to minimize tracking error and control risk. Generation III managers would diversify their portfolios across many industries and common factors. Used with intelligence, earnings-to-price ratio (E/P) tilts added 19 basis points a month on average. Because earnings revision added 50 basis points, combining these two approaches in an optimal mix was expected to add value.

However, although such a two-tilt model is a good second-generation approach, perverse periods of underperformance could occur, even if the tilts were correct, if the chosen stocks resulted in unintended effects such as high betas. The third-generation quants eliminated this risk by using an optimizer and developing a sophisticated risk model. They could then optimize their portfolios and maintain the tilts they intended while avoiding unknown bets on variability in markets or in large- or small-capitalization stocks. This dra-

matic step forward reduced the volatility of the portfolio returns, but it did not increase long-term expected returns.

All these approaches—Generations I, II, and III—have one thing in common: They assume that the historical average effectiveness of the past will continue in the future; the earnings-revision factor is twice as powerful as E/P, so the portfolio weights in the next holding period will be assigned accordingly. That approach ignores the standard deviations shown in Table 1, however, which represent the volatility of those monthly returns.

Historically, the ratio of book value to price (BV/P) has been a favorite tilt of value managers. It has added 25 basis points a month, or 3 percent a year on average for the past 18 years. However, although the tilt toward BV/P has worked well in producing more return, the volatility of these monthly returns is three times the magnitude of the mean. That is, 40 percent of the time, the reward for tilting toward BV/P has been perverse.

Rather than being resigned to periods of weak or perverse returns, which can last a year or more, the fourth-generation approach seeks to profit from volatility. By forecasting the rewards to factors (styles), Generation IV managers can make profitable shifts among them. Moreover, this approach recognizes that highly volatile factors, which were previously used primarily to control risk, offer their own rewards.

In the fourth generation, the variability in rewards is predicted for factors in a multivariate model. An optimizer is then used to tilt toward the most favorable factors while neutralizing unintended bets and minimizing tracking error. The innovation in the Generation IV model is that it recognizes the current market environment in determining each factor's weight rather than relying on average historical effectiveness.

Table 1 shows that, on average, the return to the variability-in-markets factor, which refers to stocks with high volatility in their historical returns, has been –10 basis points. The returns are to high exposure to volatility (with high defined as 1 standard deviation; the assumption is that the relationship between volatility and return is reasonably linear). Volatility of 143 basis points, which is the case for variability in markets, terrifies quants. They can be correct on all their tilts yet, unknowingly, be torpedoed because they have either a high- or low-beta portfolio. The Generation III approach could neutralize this problem by keeping the variability-in-markets exposure of a portfolio identical to that of the benchmark, but that approach overlooked 143 basis points of opportunity.

Style Forecasting

In the Generation IV models, macro-predictors can identify whether the environment is favorable or unfavorable for volatile stocks. First Quadrant's investigation into factor-return modeling concentrated on three primary areas: macromarket predictors, macroeconomic predictors, and calendar relationships.

Macromarket Predictors

Equity risk premium, stock market volatility, and recent changes in T-bill yields—all show statistical significance as predictors of factor returns. The equity risk premium, which measures how expensive the market is, is the most pervasive and interesting relationship. **Table 2** shows the correlation between some of the common factors and the equity risk premium. The equity risk premium is defined here as the trailing 12-month earnings yield (for the S&P 500) minus the T-bill rate. The correlation between the equity risk premium and variability in markets is positive. That is, volatile stocks do well if the equity risk premium is high; if the market is cheap, the equity risk premium is high and risky stocks do well. Growth, leveraged, and small-capitalization stocks also do well when equity risk premiums are high.

The rest of Table 2 presents the correlations of the factor returns with stock market variability and with cash-yield changes. Cash-yield change is defined as the change in the T-bill rate during the past month. Stock market variability is a measure of the volatility of the stock market itself during the prior six months. If the market was unusually volatile for six months, some extremely interesting relationships emerge. Once again, risk and growth do well after unusual volatility. Conservative value stocks, high-yielding stocks, do poorly on a relative basis when Treasury yields are up.

Keep in mind that these relationships are all lagged. The aim is not to forecast volatile markets or the equity risk premium; the aim is to measure

Table 2. Sensitivity of Factor Returns to Market Variables

Factor Return	Equity Risk Premium		Stock Market Variability		Cash Yield Change	
	Correlation	t-Statistic	Correlation	t-Statistic	Correlation	t-Statistic
Variability in markets	0.29	4.5	0.19	2.8	–0.14	–2.0
Success	–0.15	–2.2	–0.20	–2.9		
Size	–0.14	–2.0	–0.14	–2.0	0.15	2.2
Trading activity	0.16	2.3	0.14	2.0		
Growth exposure	0.18	2.6	0.17	2.5	–0.16	–2.3
Earnings variations			0.16	2.3	–0.13	–1.9
Financial leverage	0.13	1.9	0.20	2.9	–0.16	–2.2
Foreign income					–0.18	–2.6
Dividend yield					–0.16	–2.3

Source: First Quadrant Corp.

what the current situation is. Also, everything shown is relative; an absolute forecast is not the intent. Quants use statistics to determine if relationships are reasonably significant. That determination is difficult to make because the model violates most of the assumptions for statistical inference. Normal returns do not exist, and the error terms are not independent. Nevertheless, the model does provide information in a relative sense.

Beyond looking at interesting correlation coefficients, managers must be concerned that a relationship may be spurious. The laws of probability dictate that, in looking at lots of data, some seemingly significant relationships will be total noise. Several steps may be taken to guard against the problem of spurious relationships. The least effective is to use a hold-out period to test the relationships found in another period. Usually, this approach is the one taken, but if the analysis began with *ex post* analysis, this approach will do little to eliminate spurious relationships.

The best way to deal with spurious relationships is to apply plain common sense. Does such a relationship make sense? Common sense can be an economic or financial rationale, or it can have something to do with investor psychology. For example, a period of unusual volatility in the market is usually accompanied by investor flight to quality. Investors will oversell what they perceive to be risky—stocks with financial leverage, stocks with historically unstable earnings, small-capitalization stocks, high-beta stocks, and growth stocks. This period offers an opportunity to capture in future years value that has been rejected by nervous investors. To justify today's purchase price of a growth stock requires discounting four or five years of future earnings. When investors are nervous, they are no longer prepared to discount four or five years. Their horizons truncate to three years, two years, or one year; if they are terrified, they look only at the last quarter.

Eventually, the discount of the intrinsic growth potential for these stocks disappears. They are then remarkably cheap, and they do very well. This process takes about six months of unusual volatility. This relationship is the most pervasive First Quadrant has found. It works extremely well from the bottom up and from the top down.

Another common factor of significant interest in Table 2 is success. Success is similar to 12-month relative strength. Stocks that have done well during the past 12 months score high on success, but note that the correlations are negative. This period is one of style transition: Stocks that have done well, whether value or growth stocks, are passing on the baton of relative performance. Stocks that have done well will do poorly during the next holding period when the equity risk premium is high or when the market is volatile.

All these relationships are symmetrical. If the market is unusually stable, the opposite will hold for the next holding period. If the equity risk premium is extremely low, value will outperform with the same strength and magnitude as growth when the equity risk premium is high.

Cash-yield changes are negatively correlated with all the factor returns except size. Suppose, for example, that high-yielding stocks did poorly last month in an environment of increasing interest rates. High-yielding stocks are proxies for fixed-income investments. They do poorly as interest rates increase. Because of the lag involved, the negative correlation indicates that the rise in interest rates is not fully discounted in the price structure of high-yielding portfolios. They continue to underperform, and that information can be exploited.

Market predictors are the most useful of the three macropredictors because they are readily available and are not restated.

Macroeconomic Predictors

Producer price inflation (PPI), a proxy for general inflation, and the leading indicators also exhibit statistically significant relationships with factor returns. **Table 3** shows the sensitivity of factor returns to these economic variables. The interesting relationship here is with the common factor designated foreign income. This factor has a large negative correlation with changes in the PPI. If evidence exists of increasing inflation in the United States, stocks with exposure to foreign income will do poorly. Inflation in the United States usually means rising interest rates. With higher interest rates, the dollar usually strengthens. With a strong dollar, companies with earnings overseas are penalized by the costs of translating their earnings into strong U.S. dollars. Bear in mind, however, that these relationships are short term—one-month correlation coefficients; in the long term—a year or more—these coefficients frequently reverse signs.

Improved economic prospects, as suggested by a rise in leading economic indicators, are most helpful to companies characterized by low P/Es or high financial leverage. Conversely, a softening economy hurts these issues first.

Economic predictors are frequently restated. Thus, the manager may not know about them in time to exploit them.

Table 3. Sensitivity of Factor Returns to Economic Variables

| Factor | Percent Change in Producer Index | | Percent Change in Leading Indicators | |
	Correlation	t-Statistic	Correlation	t-Statistic
Earnings/price			0.22	3.2
Financial leverage			0.16	2.3
Labor intensity			0.16	2.3
Foreign income	−0.31	−4.6		
Yield	−0.23	−3.4		
Size	0.15	2.2		

Source: First Quadrant Corp.

Calendar Relationships

Many attributes of stock price performance exhibit significant calendar, or short-term alpha, effects. **Table 4** shows the sensitivity of factor returns to calendar effects. A stand-alone investment strategy cannot be built around calendar effects, but they are worth considering. Almost all significant January Effects are caused by taxable investors, who cause some unusual movements in stock prices in the last quarter and the first month of the year. A typical stock turns over in the United States once every two years. On average, about 4 percent of the outstanding volume trades in any given month. Taxable investors are less

Table 4. Sensitivity of Factor Returns to Calendar Effects

| Factor | Significant January Effects | | Other Significant Calendar Effects | | |
	Correlation	t-Statistic		Correlation	t-Statistic
Success	−0.33	−3.0			
Size			October	0.22	3.1
Trading activity	−0.20	−2.1			
Book/price	0.38	3.0	October	−0.23	−3.4
Earnings variation	0.27	2.5			
Dividend yield	0.24	2.4			

Source: First Quadrant Corp.

active than institutional investors, but at this time of year, they are far more active than at any other time.

As Table 4 shows, the success factor—stocks that have done well during the past 12 months—does poorly in January; the stocks typically underperform by 152 basis points in that month. Taxable investors delay realizing those gains for one month so that they will not have to pay taxes on them for another 12 months. On the margin, they have influence. No small-capitalization effect is apparent in January; because the BARRA methodology deals with a reasonably pure return to factors, any small-capitalization effect is aggregated with everything else. Stocks with high earnings variability or disappointing recent performance, illiquid issues, and high-yield issues also exhibit significant January Effects. Strong "October Effects" related to BV/P and size, and opposite to the January Effect, are also found. These effects probably result from the year-end stimuli of tax trading, window dressing, and copious information at the company level.

On average, large-capitalization stocks do better than small-capitalization stocks in October, and this tendency has been reinforced by the changes in the 1986 tax law that require mutual funds to complete their tax reporting no later than October 31. The funds want to realize losses for tax purposes, and typically, their losses are on small-capitalization, not large-capitalization, stocks. Thus, the large-capitalization effect that was already working is exaggerated.

Managers should not ignore these calendar effects. If a manager is trying to buy a stock in January that has scored high on success, he or she must be cautious and stay on the bid side. If selling that stock, the manager should be aggressive and hit the bids. High-yielding stocks usually outperform by 76 basis points in January compared with other months. If a round-trip transaction costs 100 basis points, however, chasing 76 basis points does not make sense.

Summary

Market, economic, and calendar influences do affect the future performance of various investment styles in predictable ways. The predictive power of the *ex ante* forecasts is shown in **Table 5**, which lists information coefficients for the common factors for 1980 through 1990. These figures are the correlations between the model's forecasts of the monthly return to each factor and the actual outcomes. For example, a forecast was made for stocks with high exposures to variability in markets; then at the end of the month, the return to these stocks was measured. The correlation between the two was 0.28. Information coefficients of about 0.1 pay for transaction costs, and information coefficients of about 0.3 are attractive.

Table 5. *Ex Ante* Results Summary, 1980–90

Factor	Information Coefficient	t-Statistic
Variability in markets	0.28	3.3
Success	0.41	5.1
Size	0.35	4.3
Trading activity	0.37	4.5
Growth	0.32	3.9
Earnings yield	0.46	5.9
Book/price ratio	0.37	4.5
Earnings variation	0.38	4.7
Financial leverage	0.46	5.9
Foreign income	0.38	4.7
Labor intensity	0.31	3.7
Yield	0.34	4.1
LOCAP	0.23	2.7

Source: First Quadrant Corp.

The original First Quadrant model has been expanded to include industry models based on BARRA's 55 industry classifications. The *ex ante* alpha is twice as large for the industry model as it was for the original model.

Back-Test Results

Historical models are generally unreliable as predictors of future success.

They can be used, however, to affirm the consistency and statistical significance of historical results.

Models can be tested using either *ex post* or *ex ante* data. With the *ex post* approach, the analyst builds and tests a model using historical data and known relationships. With historical data, the simulated results are generally quite good. When the models are used to manage real assets, however, the results are nowhere near as good as their indications seemed. With the *ex ante* approach, the analyst builds a model in one period and tests it in another. For example, an *ex ante* approach would build a model using data from the 1970s and see if it worked in the 1980s. Most of the time it does, because the designer of the model lived through the 1980s and knew what would probably work. An *ex ante* approach is purer than an *ex post* approach and the results are more robust, but caution is still required, and analysts must realize they will not achieve the same results with live assets.

The approach used in the test reported here is referred to as the *ex ante* expanding window. The first seven years of data, 1973 through 1979, are used to build the model and make a forecast for January 1980. At the end of January 1980, the model expands by one month, so it now has seven years and one month of historical data with which to forecast February. The model expands until it has 19 years of data to make that last forecast. This approach to testing a model is reasonably rigorous, but it is still biased because the designer of the model lived through the period.

The methodology was tested in a simulated model. The simulation was of a portfolio that was rebalanced every month using the common-factor methodology with an assumption of round-trip transaction costs amounting to 100 basis points, which is a reasonable assumption in the United States for the most liquid stocks.

Each stock in the universe of 1,000 of the most liquid stocks can be described in terms of its exposure to the common factors and its industry. This information is summarized in its alpha. These alphas range from the most negative, –40 percent, to the most positive, 40 percent. The alphas are relative to the S&P 500 return.

Figure 1 shows the value added by our simulation for the 12 years ending December 1991. For the S&P 500, 1981 and 1990 were negative years, but the value added by the simulated portfolio pulled its return into positive territory.

Figure 1. Simulated Long-Portfolio Returns, 1980–91
(net of transaction costs)

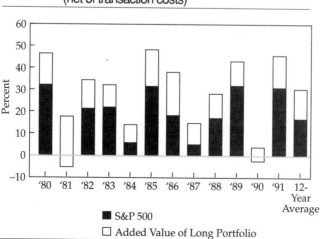

Source: First Quadrant Corp.

During that period, the return on the S&P 500 compounded nicely at 16.5 percent a year. The simulated portfolio compounded at 29.9 percent, for a value addition of 13.4 percent a year. This 13.4 percent simulated return is probably equivalent to 6.7 percent for an actual portfolio. (The rule of shaving 50 percent applies if one has a great deal of confidence in the model; if not, then shaving a higher percentage would be appropriate.)

Until recently, quants ignored stocks they expected to underperform and built portfolios around only attractive stocks. They discovered, however, that including the unattractive stocks can add value. Generally, an optimizer is used to balance a long portfolio against a benchmark such as the S&P 500 to ensure that no dramatic unknown bets are being made.

not matter, because beta is zero. This portfolio—two alphas and no beta—is thus called market neutral. If this approach is used in an environment in which the market is doing remarkably well, an S&P compounding at 17 percent a year, it can look good even though by design the strategy is negating the market.

The results of using this approach to create a hedged, market-neutral portfolio are measured against Treasury-bill returns, the appropriate benchmark, in **Figure 2**. The returns to this strategy, which compounded at 35 percent for the simulation period, outperformed the T-bill returns in every period. This performance includes a rebate that amounts to about the 8 percent compounded T-bill return. The rebate is on the short side of the portfolio.

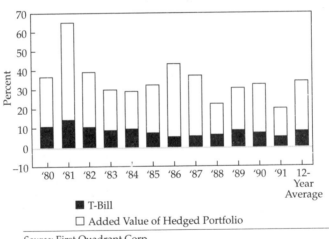

Figure 2. **Simulated Hedged-Portfolio Returns, 1980–91**
(net of transaction costs)

■ T-Bill
□ Added Value of Hedged Portfolio

Source: First Quadrant Corp.

are being made. Alternatively, an optimizer can be used to balance a short portfolio against a benchmark of unattractive stocks.

When an optimizer is used to create two portfolios—one of attractive stocks and one of unattractive stocks—in essence, the market is totally irrelevant. Whether the market is up or down and how much the market is up or down do

The simulated market-neutral portfolio is very attractive. It is a new asset class, with returns that compare favorably with those of the S&P 500 and the long-only approach, volatility somewhere between T-bills and fixed-income securities, and practically no correlation with anything else. The correlation with the return of T-bills is only 0.19, and with the equity market, –0.21.

An attractive application of the market-neutral portfolio is a long/short strategy overlaid on the S&P 500. Think of it as two alphas overlaid on the S&P 500. By going long S&P 500 futures, the strategist achieves the underlying market return overlaid with a two-tailed equity alpha. As **Figure 3** shows, if that had been done during this period, it would have given the best return because the market had such dramatic returns. What is sacrificed is the low volatility.

ured by the standard deviation of the alpha. If the standard deviation of the alpha is zero, it had zero tracking error relative to the benchmark portfolio. Tracking is not a good way to measure performance, however, because it assumes symmetry. A manager can consistently underperform the S&P 500 each month and yet have zero tracking, and the tracking error of a manager who always outperforms can be large. The only real merits of this measure are that it can identify whether a manager has

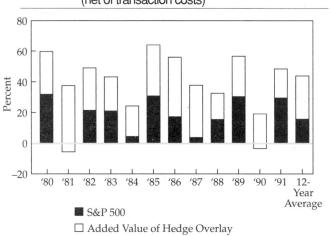

Figure 3. Returns to Simulated Index with Hedged Overlay Strategy, 1980–91
(net of transaction costs)

■ S&P 500
□ Added Value of Hedge Overlay

Source: First Quadrant Corp.

Actual Results

The performance of live portfolios is the best test of a strategy, and the available results are to be found in **Table 6**. Real returns since June 1990 were available for the long portfolio. For the first three years, this strategy outperformed the S&P 500 by about 23 percent, or by an average of 6 percent a year. The value-added returns were about half those of the simulations.

The performance of this strategy should be evaluated in terms of the risk taken to achieve the added value. One way to quantify the magnitude of the bets is to look at how well the portfolio tracked its benchmark, which is meas-

skill and it can summarize the magnitude of the bets the manager is making.

For the long portfolio, Table 6 shows that the tracking error has been a conservative 3.7 percent. On the spectrum of money managers, this error equates to about the third percentile of risk aversion, somewhere between index tilt and core managers. The return to the long portfolio was much larger than for those types of managers, however. As for consistency, on a monthly basis, the simulation worked 80 percent of the time in its simulated world, but it failed 33 percent of the time in the real world; in one month out of three, it added no value. On the quarterly level, the strategy proved to be more consistent—failing

Table 6. Real-Time Quarterly Returns, 1990–93
(net of an asset-based management fee)

		Long-Style Returns			Hedged-Style Returns		
		S&P 500	Long Style	Value Added	T-Bill	Hedged Style	Value Added
1990	June	−0.7%	−0.0%	0.7%			
	Q3	−13.8	−11.1	2.7			
	Q4	9.0	12.8	3.8			
1991	Q1	14.5	15.6	1.0			
	Q2	−0.2	0.9	1.1			
	June				0.5%	2.1%	1.6%
	Q3	5.4	8.9	3.5	1.3	5.5	4.2
	Q4	8.4	9.8	1.4	1.2	4.4	3.2
1992	Q1	−2.5	0.6	3.1	1.0	7.1	6.1
	Q2	1.9	0.7	−1.2	0.9	3.1	2.2
	Q3	3.1	1.0	−2.1	0.8	−3.1	−3.9
	Q4	5.0	5.6	0.5	0.7	2.8	2.1
1993	Q1	4.4	5.7	1.4	0.7	6.4	5.7
	Q2 (to 5/31)	0.1	0.7	0.5	0.5	0.6	0.1
Compound return		36.9	60.4	23.5	7.8	32.5	24.7
Annualized return		11.1	17.1	6.0	3.8	15.1	11.3
Annual standard deviation	13.0	12.0	3.7		5.9	5.8
Annual reward/risk		0.8	1.4	1.6		2.6	1.9
Consistency of value added							
Monthly				67.0			67.0
Quarterly				85.0			89.0

Source: First Quadrant Corp.

one quarter out of six on average.

Results with live assets for the market-neutral product were available for an even shorter time than for the long portfolio—just two years. Table 6 reveals that the T-bill, the benchmark for this strategy, returned only 7.8 percent during this time. The hedged portfolio returned 32.5 percent, for a value addition of 24.7 percent. The standard deviation is 5.9 percent, so this strategy is a low-volatility approach to managing equities.

Working through a brokerage firm would increase the costs of using this approach. In addition, although the hedged strategy would be applicable in Japan, borrowing, or shorting, securities is much more difficult in Japan than in the United States.

Ongoing Research

Recent research involves trying to predict shifts in expected rewards to each style using indexes (a top-down approach) rather than the individual stocks (a bottom-up approach). These models analyze the upcoming success of a value bias over growth, and of large stocks over small. This approach allows a portfolio to benefit from style management without incurring exposure to individual assets. The research covers the Russell, Sharpe, and Wilshire indexes, but only the results for the Wilshire will be presented here.

Wilshire Associates is a U.S. firm managing about $2 billion in four passive portfolios: large-capitalization/value, large-capitalization/growth, small-capitalization/value, and small-capitalization/growth. This firm was chosen as an example because investors can rotate their funds among the portfolios. The definition of large capitalization is determined by the top 750 stocks, and the cut-off point is about $700 million. Small capitalization includes the next 1,750 stocks, and market capitalization goes down to about $70 million. For value and growth, the definitions, which are more sophisticated than for size, involve dividend yields, P/BVs, and P/Es.

From these base series, new series were designed to dampen market exposure and better reflect style timing. The new series are Wilshire value return minus Wilshire growth return (WVG) and Wilshire large-cap-stock return minus Wilshire small-cap-stock return (WLS). Models were constructed through a three-step process. First, the predictor series were correlated against the index fund series to yield a list of likely predictors. This list was screened for financial/economic rationale and then analyzed through *ex post* multiple regressions. The final list of independent variables was refined by running *ex ante* regressions.

Economic, market, calendar, and investor-sentiment factors were used as predictors. **Table 7** shows the monthly correlations. A positive correlation coefficient means value outperforms growth; a negative correlation indicates the converse. Overall, the results of the top-down model are consistent with those of the bottom-up model.

Table 7. Wilshire Monthly Correlations, 1979–93

Variable	WVG	WLS
Economy	0.29	0.26
Interest rates	0.21	0.27
Equity risk premium	–0.26	–0.26
Market volatility	–0.14	–0.28
January	0.17	–0.13
October		0.24
WVG		0.17
WLS	0.17	
Model *ex ante* information coefficient	0.26	0.36

Source: First Quadrant Corp.

The economy has a positive correlation with value tilt, which is exactly what was found when the bottom-up approach was used. By the time it becomes obvious that the economy is doing well, it is too late to achieve superior performance, on a relative basis, by using growth stocks, so value outperforms growth. Large-cap stocks outperform small-cap stocks when the economy is obviously doing well.

When interest rates are high, value outperforms growth and large-cap stocks outperform small-cap stocks. Interestingly, this relationship holds anywhere across the maturity distribution. With the bottom-up approach, the relationship is stronger at the T-bill level; with the top-down approach, it is stronger at the longer duration. A 20-year bond was used in this model to represent interest rates, but the model would work almost as well with T-bills.

With the equity risk premium, if the market is cheap, growth outperforms value and small cap outperforms large cap. If the market has been unusually volatile, growth outperforms value and small cap outperforms large cap. These results are consistent with the findings of the bottom-up model.

January tends to be a value and small-cap month, but no evidence of this small-cap effect was found with the bottom-up approach because all the returns had been disaggregated; the research was analyzing pure returns to the BARRA factors. In the top-down approach, the returns cannot be disaggregated; the only groupings are the large-cap universe and the small-cap universe. For October, the correlation is positive, indicating that large-cap stocks outperform small-cap stocks in October.

The return to WVG is positively correlated with next month's return. This effect is referred to as positive serial correlation or autocorrelation with a one-period lag. It indicates that, if growth outperformed value last month, the odds are it will continue, and if value is outperforming, that pattern is likely to continue. The patterns do not go on indefinitely, of course, but they go on long enough to be exploitable. The *ex ante* information coefficient for the value/growth series is disappointing, although the information coefficient for the large-cap/small-cap series is good.

To test how well the model might work in the real world, First Quadrant simulated how it would work for a typical plan sponsor. The allocation guidelines among the four Wilshire funds are shown in **Table 8**. These guidelines are based on the market distribution among these styles, with some flexibility (as indicated by the minimum and maximum allocations). Because transaction costs are modest with large-cap stocks, that group is an area for flexibility in allocations. For example, if the model is forecasting a terrible scenario for large-cap value, the exposure can be reduced to 10 percent; it can only go up to 78 percent, however. Because transaction costs are so high in the small-cap stocks, less flexibility is permissible in that group; the normal allocation is 6 percent, and the range allowed is 2–10 percent. These constraints are equivalent to a 50 percent value/50 percent growth normal allocation, with 88 percent in large-cap stocks and 12 percent in small-cap stocks. The minimum allocation is at least 12 percent in value or growth, with a minimum of 80 percent in large-cap and 4 percent in small-cap stocks. The extreme position,

then, would be no more than 88 percent in value or growth, with a maximum of 96 percent in large cap and 20 percent in small cap.

The returns to the four Wilshire funds during the 10 years through December 1992 are shown in **Table 9**. The large-cap/value fund had a 16.9 percent return with 13.8 volatility; large-cap/growth outperformed large-cap/value by 100 basis points but had higher volatility. The best asset class was small-cap/value with a 21 percent return and the lowest volatility; the worst asset class was small-cap/growth with the lowest return and highest volatility.

If the plan sponsor's assets had received the market allocation shown in Table 8, the portfolio return would have been 17.3 percent with 15.1 percent volatility and 6.9 percent annual turnover because of rebalancing. Using the model to rebalance would have turned the 17.3 percent return into 19.2 percent, for a value addition of 190 basis points. The volatility would have increased from 15.1 to 15.8 percent, and annual turnover would have increased to 28.6 percent. The figure of 190 basis points is

Table 8. Management Guidelines for Tactical Style Allocation

Asset	Normal	Minimum	Maximum	Round-Trip Transaction Cost
Large value	44%	10%	78%	1%
Large growth	44	10	78	1
Small value	6	2	10	3
Small growth	6	2	10	3

Source: First Quadrant Corp.

Table 9. Tactical Style Allocation versus Multiple Managers, 1983–92

| | Wilshire Fund | | | | | | |
Item	Large-Cap/ Value	Large-Cap/ Growth	Small-Cap/ Value	Small-Cap/ Growth	Passive Sponsor: Normal	Monthly Tactical Rebalancing	Value Added
Annual return	16.9%	17.9%	21.0%	11.3%	17.3%	19.2%	1.9%
Standard deviation	13.8	17.5	13.0	22.4	15.1	15.8	2.9
Average annual turnover					6.9	28.6	

Source: First Quadrant Corp.

an *ex ante* number that should probably be cut in half to estimate actual performance. The realistic expectation would be about 100 basis points value added after transaction costs.

This method provides a tool that could be valuable to plan sponsors. Some plan sponsors have cash flows of $100 million a month to allocate. If their allocation is 60 percent equities, they must allocate $60 million a month to an existing manager. They could use this tool, among others, to help in that process. This method fails one year in four; with live assets, however, without further enhancements to the methodology, the estimated failure rate is one year in three.

Forecasting styles is dangerous, but First Quadrant's March forecasts will be discussed here to complete the information on this approach. Both one-month and six-month returns to each of the styles are forecasted. For the value/growth series, the one-month and six-month forecasts are –70 basis points and –410 basis points, respectively. The one-month forecasts are noisy, and they show no strong bias toward any particular style, although a slight bias toward growth is evident. The six-month forecast indicates that growth will outperform value stocks by about 400 basis points, although the level of significance is modest—a standard deviation of 0.4. The forecasts for large-cap/small-cap stocks are less significant, with no difference for one month and a bias of 160 basis points for small-cap over large-cap stocks for six months.

Question and Answer Session

John L. Dorian

Question: What will the fifth generation of models look like?

Dorian: The fifth generation will have something to do with artificial intelligence, although I am skeptical that artificial intelligence will add as much value as some believe. Analysts will have to be extremely cautious, because it could be the ultimate data-mining tool. It could amount to just fitting a curve, and the results might be worse than the present level of technology. The potential eventually will be realized, but not for several years. First Quadrant is experimenting with artificial intelligence and with genetic algorithms. We have not yet incorporated artificial intelligence in any sophisticated way.

Generations designate a major leap forward. Before the fifth generation arrives, fourth-generation methodologies will undergo minor enhancements. One will be to develop individual stock models. First Quadrant developed an industry model called Thrift. This industry amounts to 0.3 percent of the universe. The universe has 100 stocks larger than that. For instance, Exxon is 2.6 percent of the universe. So why not develop a model peculiar to Exxon? After stripping away Exxon's common factors and the fact that it is an international oil company, it has a company-specific error term. We are currently modeling 60 companies to determine whether we can enhance the Generation IV models by using this information.

Question: What advice do you have for people who want to use your model?

Dorian: I advise anybody using models like ours to incorporate a feedback loop. Some refer to this as an insurance policy. We use the expanding-window feedback loop. It is a slow feedback loop, however; it takes several years to have any significant influence on the relative weightings in the model. What is needed is a faster feedback loop.

Our approach also involves using the average error term during the prior 12 months to adjust next month's forecast. If the model is well specified, the errors will have a mean of zero with some variance. The expected value tells us that, whether these errors are averaged over the entire period or over 12 months, the theory holds as long as the errors have a mean of zero. If the theory holds, then using the average of the prior 12 errors to adjust next month's forecast should have no material impact on the forecast, the future performance, or the past simulation.

One way to test this proposition would be to go back and incorporate the insurance policy in the simulation: Maybe the error terms do not average zero over short periods. In almost all cases, our tests of this insurance added no value at all.

This approach is an example of an insurance policy for something one hopes will never happen. The model is built over the most recent 20 years, however; it has not gone through some environments that will be faced in the future, and the expanding window will take too long to recognize these environments. For example, we have a forecast for companies with high exposure to foreign income. If we go into an environment of protectionism in the United States, our methodology for forecasting foreign income may be noisy or even perverse. With an insurance feedback loop of the average of the most recent 12 error terms, a correction starts taking place after about six months.

Question: In the short term, the forecast could be very erratic, but in the long term, growth and value could wash each other out, resulting in minimal impact for either. What is the optimal forecasting horizon?

Dorian: We are constantly concerned about the optimal holding period. We have conducted various experiments involving transaction costs using different holding periods to determine the optimal holding period. If you have two options that are close, then go with the lower turnover scenario, because transacting entails cost. We have noise associated with our alpha, but the inefficiencies in the U.S. market are far less obvious now than before. Quants have much more difficulty earning their alphas. If a quant adds 200 basis points a year, she or he is doing a remarkably good job.

We must turn our attention to short-fuse alphas, because holding periods are shorter. I believe the optimal holding period should be three months. That does not mean you turn over 100 percent every three months, but one model should have a three-month holding period to determine the structure of the portfolio and another should have a one-month holding period to influence implementation. To reduce turnover, the three-month model should emphasize the positive serial correlation of the forecast. Some of the information coefficient should be sacrificed to increase the autocorrelation of the forecast. Doing so will lower the turnover and enhance the model's timeliness by concentrating on a three-month period.

For example, I described the inefficiencies that arose with earnings-revision data. Five years ago, that could have been exploited with three-month

old information. Today, the most pervasive inefficiency is unusual market volatility during the past six months. Possibly a year from now, the exploitable period may be during the past three months instead of six because others observe the inefficiency and start to exploit it. Quants need to front-run other quants and use models that are practical, even if they are less statistically significant, because those models will result in higher realized returns. The example of market volatility could be relevant. In analyzing the past 20 years, the relationship with market volatility measured over six months dominates the relationship measured over three months, but the 20-year period must be split into subsets.

The information in the most recent five years will provide clues as to what is happening. The shifting of what was a six-month inefficiency to a three-month inefficiency is a clue that others are arbitraging away your inefficiency. To capture wealth, you must be prepared to shift gears and go with a lower statistical information coefficient.

Question: How frequently should the portfolio be tactically rebalanced?

Dorian: Differences in rebalancing frequency produce different results, which is one reason for being skeptical of simulations. Some simulations use more rigorous implementation assumptions than others. An aggressive simulation implements the entire flexibility of the range at a lower signal—a 1-sigma as opposed to a 2-sigma signal. The assets of this simulation are 100 percent invested and turnover is much higher, but it will cost more to implement. Factoring in accurate turnover costs will reduce the realized gain. The simulation I presented was one of the high-turnover simulations but certainly not the highest.

Equity Securities Analysis in the United States: Its Experience and Future

Frederick L. Muller, CFA
President
Atlanta Capital Management Company

Professional securities analysis in the United States began in the 1920s, and its evolution was accelerated by the extreme volatility of the stock market in the 1930s. A second period of great change followed the introduction of quantitative methods in the 1970s. The next frontier may be the application of nonlinear systems.

Truly seminal ideas about approaches to investing occur infrequently, and then, only during a period of extreme financial adversity do these ideas take root and achieve widespread application among practitioners. These observations are confirmed by the history of securities analysis in the United States.

History of Securities Analysis

The first real evidence of any kind of professional approach to securities analysis in the United States comes from the 1920s. At that time, people studied the numbers and attempted to value assets based on sparse public information. Insiders supplemented the public information with private knowledge, which aided in creating wealth for many people during the roaring bull market of the 1920s. The individuals who labored with these numbers were called statisticians and were somewhat visible in the investment process, although their role was greatly limited. Nevertheless, this decade saw the beginnings of profes-

sional securities analysis.

The devastation of the capital markets in the 1930s accelerated the development of securities analysis. The seminal ideas about how securities analysts practice the craft, even to this day, were articulated during this decade. The stock market declined 86 percent from its peak in September 1929 to its low point in June 1932, and it continued on a roller-coaster ride for the next several years. From its 1932 low, the market rose by 322 percent through March 1937 but remained 41 percent below its 1929 peak. Another slide of 54 percent took place in 1938; then, the market rose again by 56 percent in 1939. The Dow Jones Industrial Average, however, did not exceed its 1929 peak until the early 1950s. The 1930s were a period of remarkable and unprecedented volatility in the capital markets and forever changed the way money in the United States is invested.

At the national level, social policy in the 1930s reaffirmed the basic tenet that public markets are essential to the effective functioning of free-market economies and that "the greatest social good" can be achieved only by having open and honest capital markets. The notion of "disclosure" became the centerpiece of national legislation requiring the public availability of corporate financial information. Failure to disclose relevant financial information in dealing with investors made corporations and their investment bankers liable to serious court proceedings.

The most important legislation was the Securities Act of 1933 and the Securities Exchange Act of 1934. Both acts were administered by the Securities and Exchange Commission, established soon after the acts' passage. From this time forward, the corporate financial information made available to investors for their examination before making investment decisions was more extensive and more accurate than in the past.

The availability of information created a need for a coherent framework for analyzing financial statements. In 1934, this framework appeared in an immensely important book written by Benjamin Graham and David Dodd.[1] Although *Security Analysis* was not a book on theory, it offered a rigorous approach to a fundamental examination of the worth of a company's balance sheet and earning power. Graham and Dodd also formulated criteria for selecting specific common stocks for investment purposes. The ideas presented were not only sensible and intelligent but also very practical in application. This book, still held in high esteem, is considered by many to be the bible of fundamental company research.

The other profoundly important book in this decade was by John Burr Williams.[2] Williams was the first to lay out in equation form the theory for discounting future cash flows to their present value as a technique for determining the worth of a common stock. His Rule of Present Worth is so powerful that it still endures as the essence of dividend discount models widely used by practitioners of securities analysis around the world.

Other significant concepts emerged during this idea-rich decade. For instance, in *The General Theory of Employment, Interest and Money*, John Maynard Keynes discussed "the state of long-term expectations."[3] Keynes dealt with uncertainty in forecasting prospective returns on investments, a concept that remains a perplexity in modern-day securities analysis. Also during this period, Frederick R. Macaulay defined the concept of duration, or the weighted-average time to maturity of the present value of interest and principal payments of a loan or bond.[4] Although duration is used mainly in the analysis of bonds, it is also an important addition to the literature on valuing common stocks. A final example of the wealth of ideas in the 1930s was the publication of T. Rowe Price's *Picking "Growth" Stocks*.[5] Interest in growth-stock investing is not merely a phenomenon of recent years; Price laid out the principles of it more than half a century ago.

From these seminal ideas born in the difficult economic and financial decade of the 1930s, we began after World War II to build the securities analysis profession. Particularly noteworthy during the 1950s and 1960s was the ascent of institutional research. In the late 1950s, several pioneering brokerage firms built their businesses on producing detailed, lengthy analyses of companies. Those reports were then sold to bank trust departments, mutual funds, and investment counselors for use in making their

---

[1] *Security Analysis* (New York: McGraw-Hill, 1934).

[2] *The Theory of Investment Value* (Cambridge, Mass.: Harvard University Press, 1938).

[3] (New York: Harcourt, Brace, 1936).

[4] *Some Theoretical Problems Suggested by the Movement of Interest Rates, Bond Yields and Stock Prices in the United States since 1856* (New York: National Bureau of Economic Research, 1938).

[5] (Princeton, N.J.: Barron's, 1939):3–18.

investment decisions. Some of the most successful of these firms were Drexel & Company; H.C. Wainwright; Donaldson, Lufkin & Jenrette; and Faulkner, Dawkins & Sullivan. What developed as institutional research in these decades had the effect of impounding fundamental analysis into an investment decision-making approach that was more objective and professional than previous approaches.

By the early 1960s, the viability of this profession was unquestionable. In 1962, the Financial Analysts Federation gave birth to the Institute of Chartered Financial Analysts for the purpose of testing professional analysts on their knowledge of the theory and application of objective analysis of investment opportunities and for certifying successful examinees as Chartered Financial Analysts. The CFA designation formalized securities analysis into a highly respected profession.

Before turning to the second period of significant change since the 1920s, let us recall the objectives of securities analysis as stated by Graham and Dodd in their 1962 edition of *Security Analysis*: First, securities analysis seeks to present the important facts about a publicly held corporate stock or bond issue in a manner most informing and useful to an actual or potential owner; second, securities analysis seeks to reach dependable conclusions, based on the facts and applicable standards, as to the safety and attractiveness of a given security at the current market price or some assumed future price.[6] The 1970s ushered in a decade of significant change in the way securities analysis is performed; yet the new quantitative techniques continued to fit the objectives stated by Graham and Dodd in 1962 and defined years earlier.

What stimulated the 1970s' dramatic change in the way long-term capital is invested? The convergence of three powerful forces in the financial markets made change inevitable. First, the ideas embraced in what is broadly termed modern portfolio theory (MPT) became increasingly available within the professional literature. Moreover, these ideas became increasingly easy to implement in actual portfolios because of cheap computing power and simple models. Second, the amount of assets flowing to professional investment management institutions exploded. These assets came primarily from pension funds, which were prompted (in part, by the 1974 passage of the Employee Retirement Income Security Act) to strengthen the viability of the private pension system. Third, after the bear market of 1970 and an even worse devastation of wealth in 1973 and 1974, disappointment about the ability of any investment manager to earn excess returns became pervasive.

The concepts underlying MPT can be traced back to French mathematician Louis Bachelier at the turn of the century. In his dissertation, "The Theory of Speculation,"[7] Bachelier applied theory, including mathematics, to the behavior of the stock market.

The next great contribution was the work of Harry Markowitz.[8] He believed that "portfolio analysis starts with information concerning individual securities. It ends with conclusions concerning portfolios as a whole. The purpose of the analysis is to find portfolios which best meet the objectives of the investor." Markowitz started with the premise that an investor needs information on individual securities, whether the information is the historical return and risk performance of stocks or the forecasts of securities analysts about the expected return and risk. When using the analysts' inputs, investor portfolios reflect the analysts' beliefs. From the begin-

---

[6]Benjamin Graham, David Dodd, and Sidney Cottle, *Security Analysis: Principles and Techniques*, 4th ed. (New York: McGraw-Hill, 1962).

[7]Reprinted in P. Cootner, *The Random Character of Stock Market Prices* (Cambridge, Mass.: MIT Press, 1964).

[8]"Portfolio Selection," *The Journal of Finance* (March 1952):77–91.

ning of MPT, the role of securities analysts was important in building portfolios to satisfy investors at their preferred levels of risk, which kept alive the hope for active management as a way to outperform indexes, at least on a risk-adjusted basis.

The next great advance in MPT came with the publication of William Sharpe's paper on the capital asset pricing model.[9] The CAPM was the breakthrough needed to allow the ideas of modern financial theory to be applied to real-life portfolios in a cost-effective way.

The development of modern financial theory is a fascinating history, which has been recorded by Peter Bernstein in his recent book, *Capital Ideas: The Improbable Origins of Modern Wall Street*.[10] Not only does Bernstein humanize the contributors to this newly significant branch of economics, called "financial economics," but he also skillfully integrates the different concepts developed by individual contributors. Thus, he demonstrates the continuity and interdependence of these ideas in the progress of the overall theory. Adding legitimacy to the validity of financial economics was the awarding of the 1990 Nobel Prize in economics to Harry Markowitz, Merton Miller, and William Sharpe.

The theory and mathematical techniques used in the application of MPT were well suited to the large amounts of pension monies flowing into institutions for long-term investment, especially in the use of index funds, which had their commercial birth in the 1970s. Index funds and passive management developed from a slow beginning that was prompted by disappointment with active investment performance. Diminished confidence in active management

was exacerbated by the loss of 71 percent in the real purchasing power of stock prices from the market peak in 1966 through the summer of 1982, when the great bull market began. Similar to the experience in the 1930s, adversity in the markets opened the door for new theory ushering in change in practitioners' approaches to investing. Passive management and index funds grew into an important force that changed the face of the investment management industry.

The 1970s provided the opportunity for modern analysts to make widespread use of computers in analyzing income statements and balance sheets. Analysts could now manipulate a greater amount of information quicker and more cheaply than ever before. Quantitative models developed to forecast company growth rates, when coupled with dividend discount models, allowed the modern analyst to rank individual securities on the quality of the fundamental earnings forecast and attractiveness of the stock. These lists of securities were fed into optimizers to create portfolios at specified risk levels. In active-management organizations, the need for securities analysis did not diminish, but it was practiced quite differently from the ways of the 1950s and 1960s. Nevertheless, Graham and Dodd's definition of the objectives of securities analysis continued to guide the profession.

The 1980s saw the full flowering of quantitative techniques. Passive management grew in importance, and by the late 1980s, approximately a third of institutional assets were indexed. Tilt funds, which fall somewhere between traditional active management and passive management, came into widespread use. The absolute and relative number of analysts practicing securities analysis in the traditional manner of the 1950s and 1960s shrank as those using quantitative methods increased.

---

[9]"Capital Asset Prices: A Theory of Market Equilibriums under Conditions of Risk," *The Journal of Finance* (September 1964).

[10](New York: Maxwell MacMillan International, 1992).

Securities Analysis Today

This evolution of the art and science of securities analysis has brought us to the current state of our profession. Although passive management appears to have peaked momentarily in the United States, it will remain important. Is there, then, hope for active management? Why do so many investors continue to pursue excess returns despite the considerable evidence that they are very difficult to earn? The answer, very simply, is that when most analysts look at the behavior of markets, they cannot resist the temptation to try to beat them.

For instance, **Figure 1** shows the behavior of four stock market indexes from 1980 through the end of 1992. The returns shown are cumulative annual returns based on price changes only, excluding dividends. They are presented as they would appear to a yen-based investor. Certain markets seem to do well for several years and then poorly. Not only that, each index is volatile in and of itself. Despite what has happened since 1989, the Nikkei Index accumulated the best return during those 12 years.

After observing the annual returns

Figure 1. Market Return Measured in Yen: Selected Indexes, 1981–92

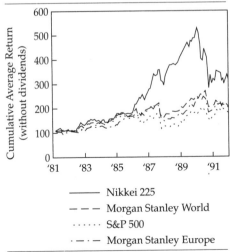

——— Nikkei 225
– – – Morgan Stanley World
······ S&P 500
· – · – Morgan Stanley Europe

Source: Atlanta Capital Management Co., based on data from Asset Investment Management.

of each index during this period and the associated standard deviations, shown in **Figure 2**, an investor's impulse to attempt to manage portfolios actively in order to squeeze out excess returns is very powerful: "If only I could take advantage of this volatility, I could earn excess returns." Notice that the Nikkei, the S&P 500, and the Morgan Stanley Europe indexes have volatility measures of 19 to 20 percent. As MPT suggests, when those indexes are combined into a world index, the return goes down slightly but so does the risk (as measured by the standard deviation).

Figure 2. Market Return and Standard Deviation Measured in Yen: Selected Indexes

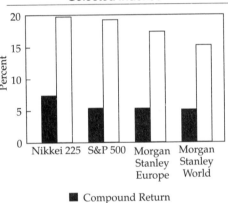

■ Compound Return
□ Standard Deviation

Source: Atlanta Capital Management Co., based on data from Asset Investment Management.

Does any theory and/or evidence suggest that the most important finding of the CAPM—namely, that under equilibrium market conditions, an investor cannot earn excess returns for an assumed level of risk—is flawed enough to justify the practice of active management? The CAPM is increasingly under attack because pieces of evidence indicate that the theory does not hold under all circumstances. An example of a niche in the market that has not been completely exploited is the January Effect, but others exist. A recent study by Fama and French comes down hard on the assertion that beta is a reliable predictor of risk and that expected returns are positively related to beta risk.[11] According to Fama and French, higher returns appear to be more a function of small size and lower valuation, as represented by price to book value, than of beta. The evidence against the efficacy of the CAPM is still drifting in, but it is not overwhelming.

The CAPM is also under attack at the level of fundamental theory. In a recent unpublished paper, Mordecai Kurz of Stanford University argues that market participants, even though they share the same information, hold different beliefs about how future events will unfold.[12] In the CAPM, however, a crucial assumption is that all information is immediately reflected in stock prices, which allows no single market participant to gain a consistent advantage over others and thereby obtain excess returns.

If Kurz is correct, there may yet be hope for active management based on superior securities analysis, because even though investors have the same information, individual investors will draw different rational conclusions, based on their beliefs, about that information. Acting separately on their own rational tenets, investors misprice stocks, as in the case of the crash in 1987. According to Kurz, the reason for the mispricing is that investors make incorrect assessments of the future, even though they have rationally processed all known information. By inference, Kurz asserts that those investors who can make correct assessments of future events can earn excess returns by taking advantage of mispricing.

Future Securities Analysis

The human mind craves clairvoyance,

but anyone's ability to see the future is extremely limited. Nevertheless, some trends are already in place that promise to persist well into this decade. For instance, under the purview of fundamental analysis, the opportunity exists in the United States to use traditional securities analysis to uncover excess returns among small companies. Because of the success of passive management, the research performed on some of these small companies is minimal or virtually nonexistent. Collecting and analyzing little-known information on small companies with the objective of discovering mispricing could be a fruitful activity.

Another promising application of fundamental analysis is to shift analytical focus from the more traditional emphasis on forecasting future earnings to other ways of identifying companies' financial potential. For example, G. Bennett Stewart III has made a strong argument for analyzing and valuing companies based on their cash flow characteristics rather than accounting earnings.[13]

In the realm of quantitative models, most sophisticated investment management organizations relentlessly pursue improvements. The objective is to use more or better information, or both, to uncover stocks that sell below the values imputed by their models. Better inputs might be defined as those allowing an investor to gain a short-term advantage, such as being quicker than others to recognize revisions in consensus earnings estimates, or inputs of a longer term nature, such as national or international economic trends and the effect of those trends on a particular industry or company. Model building is fascinating and leads to insights that less precise analytical methods might miss.

Perhaps the next period of severe adversity in the financial markets will bring forth a new set of ideas as the 1930s and 1970s did. If and when that will

[11]Eugene F. Fama and Kenneth R. French, "The Cross-Section of Expected Stock Returns," *The Journal of Finance* (June 1992):427–65.

[12]"Asset Prices with Rational Beliefs." My exposure to Professor Kurz's work is through the courtesy of Dr. Woody Brock of Strategic Economic Decisions, Menlo Park, Calif., in his *Forecast* service, 1993. When the Kurz paper is published, we will be able to examine it in detail.

[13]*The Quest for Value* (New York: HarperCollins, 1991).

happen is impossible to foretell. Perhaps the most promising theory for further practical application falls under the description of nonlinear systems. The CAPM and its associated theory and application rely on linear mathematics, an approach bequeathed to financial economics from the physical sciences, in which relationships are far more constant than in a social phenomenon such as the stock market. Through observation, through the study of the biological sciences, investigators intuitively know that complex relationships in human systems are nonlinear. Complex organic systems learn and adapt to structural changes in their environments. Indeed, that is how they survive.

Investment applications of nonlinear mathematics, however, must await further development of mathematical techniques that allow us to create new models that more accurately describe the inner workings of the stock market than do the old models. One point seems increasingly clear with respect to the stock market: It adapts to change in a nonlinear manner. Nonlinear mathematical techniques will change the practice of securities analysis dramatically even though the objective of that analysis will remain the same: to evaluate the relationship between value and price.

Chaos theory is probably closer to practical development than some of the exotic approaches, such as the use of genetic algorithms, neural networks, and so forth. Chaos theory is finding adherents in Japan among companies such as Hitachi, which is selling software to help forecast the stock market.

The most fruitful area for future research is in these nonlinear approaches, but researchers are a long way from developing the financial theory and tools necessary to apply this approach effectively to investing. Mitchell Waldrop, in his book on this quest for nonlinear approaches, describes the activities of the Santa Fe Institute, a collection of scientists, economists, and other deep thinkers engaged in this effort.[14]

An Example of Securities Analysis

For most active managers, securities analysis is an attempt to integrate traditional securities analysis with modern financial tools in order to earn excess returns. As an example of this process, I will use my firm's process of investment selection, which is illustrated in **Figure 3**. The first element of this process is the restriction of investment opportunities to a defined high-quality

[14]*Complexity: The Emerging Sciences at the Edge of Order and Chaos* (New York: Simon & Schuster, 1992).

Figure 3. Equity Selection Process

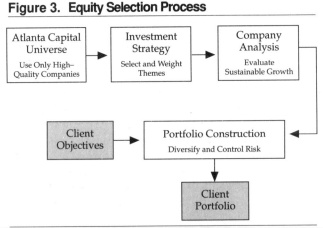

Source: Atlanta Capital Management Co.

universe of companies that meet certain quality and liquidity criteria. Essentially, these companies have a 10-year history of growth and stability in earnings and dividends and the expectation that these basic trends will continue. The stocks must be liquid enough to allow accumulation of large positions and trading in an amount, on average, of at least $500,000 a day in market value, as measured for the past 60 days.

The next element in the process is investment strategy. At Atlanta Capital, we attempt to identify long-term (three- to five-year) themes of a macro nature with trends that will favorably affect the businesses of companies in which we want to invest. For instance, we believe that capital investment will be more important in the United States during the next few years than during the 1980s, which will favorably affect companies operating in the capital investment sector of the economy.

The next step in our process is to analyze these economically favored companies by focusing on their sustainable growth (the internal growth rate, or retention rate of earnings times the return on equity) to identify those expected to be above average during the next several years. **Table 1, Table 2, Table 3,** and **Table 4** illustrate how we evaluate this sustainable growth rate. Safety-Kleen, the focus of this illustration, is a leading medium-sized company in the waste materials business. Table 1 contains our assumptions for the company's sales, profitability, and financing needs based on the values of these variables for the past five years.

In working through the forecast for the income statement and balance sheet, we determined the financing the company will need in order to meet its growth objectives and thereby arrive at a forecast for the sustainable growth rate of the company during the next five years. We obtained management's help in deriving these forecasts, but the process does not in any way include the traditional earnings per share forecasts.

Our focus is on long-term fundamentals of the business as the company might view them internally.

Based on Safety-Kleen's sales growth through the end of 1991, we made forecasts of the growth rate of sales five years into the future. For this company, growth slowed in 1987 and 1988 because of the recession; at the end of 1991, the growth rate was 18 percent. As a result of this slowdown, the cost of goods sold (COGS) and selling, general, and administrative (SG&A) expenses rose as a percentage of sales. One of the interesting things about Safety-Kleen is that depreciation and amortization (D&A) increased dramatically during the past several years because of the company's investments, primarily in building new plants in Europe in order to support future sales growth. We do not believe that level of investment will persist, so in our five-year forecast, depreciation drops back to a percentage that is near the 1988 level.

Table 2 illustrates how these percentages translate into dollars in the income statement, beginning with a sales forecast we make for the company based on the assumptions in Table 1. The last line in Table 2 shows the percentage change in net income each year. The company had negative growth in 1991, but that growth is expected to return to normal during the next five years. Because net income has been reduced so much, the percentage increases as the company resumes growth are quite large.

We use the same approach for the balance sheet, as shown in Table 3 and Table 4. We are not trying to forecast every one of the items on the balance sheet with great precision, but this framework provides a discipline for the forecasting process. If our assumptions are flawed, of course, these numbers may not make sense.

The important figures on the balance sheet are the forecasts of stockholders' equity and financing needed. "Extra financing needed" means the com-

Table 1. Calculations and Assumptions for Pro Forma Income Statement: Safety-Kleen Company

Item	Actual					+1 Year	Estimated			
	01/02/88	12/31/88	12/30/89	12/29/90	12/28/91		+2 Years	+3 Years	+4 Years	+5 Years
Sales growth	30.7%	25.0%	14.6	23.2%	18.0	17.0%	18.0%	18.0%	18.0%	18.0%
COGS/sales	60.0	63.8	62.9	62.1	62.9	62.5	62.2	62.0	62.0	62.0
SG&A/sales	15.3	14.4	13.9	13.8	14.4	14.3	14.0	13.7	13.3	13.0
D&A/sales	6.7	6.8	7.1	7.9	8.7	8.5	8.2	7.5	7.0	6.5
Interest expense/sales	0.4	0.8	1.8	2.0	1.9	1.8	1.7	1.6	1.6	1.5
Equity in earnings (subsidiaries)/sales	0.0	0.0	0.0	0.0	0.0	0.0	0.0	0.0	0.0	0.0
Other income/sales	0.5	0.4	0.7	0.6	0.3	0.4	0.4	0.5	0.5	0.5
Other expense/sales	0.0	0.0	0.0	0.0	0.4	0.4	0.4	0.4	0.4	0.4
Pretax minority interest/sales	0.0	0.0	0.0	0.0	0.0	0.0	0.0	0.0	0.0	0.0
Tax rate	42.1	36.5	36.1	36.8	38.2	38.0	38.0	38.0	38.0	38.0
Special items/sales	0.0	0.0	0.0	0.0	0.0	0.0	0.0	0.0	0.0	0.0
After-tax minority interest/sales	0.0	0.0	0.0	0.0	0.0	0.0	0.0	0.0	0.0	0.0
Preferred dividends ($millions)	$0.0	$0.0	$0.0	$0.0	$0.0	$0.0	$0.0	$0.0	$0.0	$0.0
Common dividend payout ratio	22.6%	25.9%	26.5%	25.5%	35.3%	30.0%	27.0%	22.0%	20.0%	18.0%

Source: Atlanta Capital Management Co., based on data from Value Line.

Table 2. Pro Forma Income Statement: Safety-Kleen Company
(dollars in millions)

Item	Actual					Estimated				
	01/02/88	12/31/88	12/30/89	12/29/90	12/28/91	+1 Year	+2 Years	+3 Years	+4 Years	+5 Years
Net sales	$334	$417	$478	$589	$695	$813	$960	$1,132	$1,336	$1,577
COGS	200	266	301	366	437	508	597	702	828	977
SG&A	51	60	66	81	100	116	134	155	178	205
Operating income before depreciation	$83	$91	$111	$142	$157	$189	$228	$275	$330	$394
D&A	22	28	34	46	60	69	79	85	94	102
Interest	1	3	8	12	13	15	16	18	21	24
+Equity in earnings (subsidiaries)	0	0	0	0	0	0	0	0	0	0
+Other income	2	2	3	3	2	3	4	6	7	8
Other expenses	0	0	0	0	3	3	4	5	5	6
+Pretax minority interest	0	0	0	0	0	0	0	0	0	0
Pretax income	61	61	72	87	83	105	133	173	216	270
Income taxes (total)	26	22	26	32	32	40	51	66	82	102
+Special items	0	0	0	0	0	0	0	0	0	0
+After-tax minority interest	0	0	0	0	0	0	0	0	0	0
Net income	$ 35	$ 39	$ 46	$ 55	$ 52	$ 65	$ 83	$ 107	$ 134	$ 167
Preferred dividends	0	0	0	0	0	0	0	0	0	0
Net income available for common dividends	35	39	46	55	52	65	83	107	134	167
Common dividends	8	10	12	14	18	20	22	24	27	30
Income in retained earnings before adjustments	27	29	34	41	33	46	60	84	107	137
Change in net income	37%	10%	19%	20%	-7%	26%	27%	30%	25%	25%

Source: Atlanta Capital Management Co., based on data from Value Line.

Table 3. Calculations and Assumptions for Pro Forma Balance Sheet: Safety-Kleen Company
(dollars in millions)

Item	Actual					Estimated				
	01/02/88	12/31/88	12/30/89	12/29/90	12/28/91	+1 Year	+2 Years	+3 Years	+4 Years	+5 Years
Cash/sales	5.3%	9.0%	4.9%	5.6%	2.9%	3.0%	3.0%	3.0%	3.0%	3.0%
Accounts receivable/sales	13.4	12.9	14.9	15.0	14.7	14.5	14.0	14.0	14.0	13.5
Inventory/sales	7.6	5.9	6.3	5.5	5.7	6.0	5.8	5.6	5.5	5.5
Other current assets/sales	2.1	2.0	3.0	2.7	2.9	3.0	3.0	3.0	3.0	3.0
Net plant/sales	57.5	59.9	73.3	81.2	86.8	86.0	80.0	72.0	64.0	56.0
Long-term investments	$ 0.0	$ 0.0	$ 0.0	$ 0.0	$ 0.0	$ 0.0	$ 0.0	$ 0.0	$ 0.0	$ 0.0
Deferred charges	0.0	0.0	0.0	0.0	0.0	0.0	0.0	0.0	0.0	0.0
Intangibles	0.0	0.0	36.0	54.0	107.0	107.0	107.0	107.0	107.0	107.0
Other long-term assets	16.0	25.0	13.0	17.0	11.0	11.0	11.0	11.0	11.0	11.0
Notes payable	0.0	0.0	0.0	0.0	0.0	0.0	0.0	0.0	0.0	0.0
Debt in current liabilities	1.0	1.0	2.0	2.0	15.0	15.0	15.0	15.0	15.0	15.0
Accounts payable/sales	5.3%	6.9%	7.1%	7.9%	6.9%	7.0%	7.0%	7.0%	7.0%	7.0%
Taxes payable/sales	1.6	1.8	0.7	1.4	1.3	1.4	1.4	1.4	1.4	1.4
Other current liabilities/ sales	7.0	8.1	8.8	7.7	8.0	7.5	7.0	7.0	7.0	7.0
Total long-term debt	$28.0	$61.0	$138.0	$122.0	$244.0	$314.0	$336.0	$315.0	$267.0	$174.0
Deferred tax and investment tax credit	36.0	37.0	44.0	51.0	56.0	55.0	55.0	55.0	55.0	55.0
Minority interest	0.0	0.0	0.0	0.0	0.0	0.0	0.0	0.0	0.0	0.0
Other long-term liabilities	8.0	13.0	13.0	13.0	12.0	12.0	12.0	12.0	12.0	12.0
Preferred equity	0.0	0.0	0.0	0.0	0.0	0.0	0.0	0.0	0.0	0.0
Common stock	3.0	3.0	3.0	6.0	6.0	6.0	6.0	6.0	6.0	6.0
Treasury stock	0.0	0.0	0.0	0.0	0.0	0.0	0.0	0.0	0.0	0.0
Unreconciled	2.0	3.0	2.0	6.0	2.0	0.0	0.0	0.0	0.0	0.0

Source: Atlanta Capital Management Co., based on data from Value Line.

Table 4. Pro Forma Balance Sheet: Safety-Kleen Company
(dollars in millions)

Item	Actual					Estimated				
	01/02/88	12/31/88	12/30/89	12/29/90	12/28/91	+1 Year	+2 Years	+3 Years	+4 Years	+5 Years
Assets										
Cash and equivalents	$ 18	$ 37	$ 24	$ 33	$ 20	$ 24	$ 29	$ 34	$ 40	$ 47
Accounts receivable	45	54	71	89	102	118	134	159	187	213
Inventories	25	25	30	32	40	49	56	63	73	87
Other current assets	7	8	14	16	20	24	29	34	40	47
Total current assets	94	124	139	170	182	215	248	290	341	394
Net plant	192	250	351	478	603	699	768	815	855	883
Long-term investments	0	0	0	0	0	0	0	0	0	0
Deferred charges	0	0	0	0	0	0	0	0	0	0
Intangibles	0	0	36	54	107	107	107	107	107	107
Other long-term assets	16	25	13	17	11	11	11	11	11	11
Total assets	$302	$399	$538	$719	$904	$1,033	$1,133	$1,223	$1,314	$1,395
Liabilities										
Notes payable	0	0	0	0	0	0	0	0	0	0
Debt in current liabilities	1	1	2	2	15	15	15	15	15	15
Accounts payable	18	29	34	47	48	57	67	79	94	110
Taxes payable	5	8	3	9	9	11	13	16	19	22
Other current liabilities	23	34	42	46	56	61	67	79	94	110
Total current liabilities	48	71	82	103	128	144	163	189	221	258
Total long-term debt	28	61	138	122	244	314	336	315	267	174
Deferred tax and investment tax credit	36	37	44	51	56	55	55	55	55	55
Minority interest	0	0	0	0	0	0	0	0	0	0
Other long-term liabilities	8	13	13	13	12	12	12	12	12	12
Total liabilities	$120	$182	$277	$289	$440	$ 525	$ 566	$ 571	$ 555	$ 499
Preferred stock	0	0	0	0	0	0	0	0	0	0
Common stock	3	3	3	6	6	6	6	6	6	6
Additional paid-in capital	25	28	39	161	165	165	165	165	165	165
Earned surplus	151	182	216	257	290	336	396	480	587	724

Table continued on page 58.

Table 4. Pro Forma Balance Sheet: Safety-Kleen Company (Continued)
(millions of dollars)

Item	Actual					Estimated				
	01/02/88	12/31/88	12/30/89	12/29/90	12/28/91	+1 Year	+2 Years	+3 Years	+4 Years	+5 Years
Treasury stock	$ 0	$ 0	$ 0	$ 0	$ 0	$ 0	$ 0	$ 0	$ 0	$ 0
Unreconciled	2	3	2	6	2	0	0	0	0	0
Common equity	182	216	261	430	464	507	568	651	759	896
Total stockholders' equity	182	216	261	430	464	507	568	651	759	896
Total liabilities and equity	$302	$399	$538	$719	$904	$1,033	$1,133	$1,223	$1,313	$1,395
Extra financing needed (negative value indicates extra cash)						0	0	0	0	0
Adjusted total liabilities and equity after financing needs						1,033	1,133	1,223	1,314	1,395
Sustainable growth	15%	13%	13%	10%	7%	9%	11%	13%	14%	15%

Source: Atlanta Capital Management Co., based on data from Value Line.

Table 5. DuPont Analysis: Safety-Kleen Company

Item	Actual					Estimated				
	01/02/88	12/31/88	12/30/89	12/29/90	12/28/91	+1 Year	+2 Years	+3 Years	+4 Years	+5 Years
Sales, net	100.0%	100.0%	100.0%	100.0%	100.0%	100.0%	100.0%	100.0%	100.0%	100.0%
COGS	60.0	63.8	62.9	62.1	62.9	62.5	62.2	62.0	62.0	62.0
SG&A	15.3	14.4	13.9	13.8	14.4	14.3	14.0	13.7	13.3	13.0
D&A	6.7	6.8	7.1	7.9	8.7	8.5	8.2	7.5	7.0	6.5
Interest	0.4	0.8	1.8	2.0	1.9	1.8	1.7	1.6	1.6	1.5
+/− Other	0.5	0.4	0.7	0.6	−0.1	0.0	0.0	0.1	0.1	0.1
Income, pretax sales	18.2	14.5	15.1	14.8	12.0	12.9	13.9	15.3	16.2	17.1
1 − Tax rate	57.9	63.5	63.9	63.2	61.8	62.0	62.0	62.0	62.0	62.0
Total assets/common equity	1.7	1.8	2.1	1.7	2.0	2.0	2.0	1.9	1.7	1.6
Sales/total assets	1.1	1.1	0.9	0.8	0.8	0.8	0.9	0.9	1.0	1.1
1 − Payout ratio	0.8	0.7	0.7	0.8	0.7	0.7	0.7	0.8	0.8	0.8
Sustainable growth	14.9%	13.2%	13.0%	9.6%	7.2%	9.0%	10.6%	12.9%	14.1%	15.3%

Source: Atlanta Capital Management Co., based on data from Value Line.

pany does not have the profitability to meet its sales growth targets with the balance sheet it has. In that case, the company must go to the market to sell bonds or equity or to the bank to borrow money in order to realize its growth targets. Ambitious plans for growth must make sense when the extra financing needs are considered. The last line of Table 4 shows our estimate of Safety-Kleen's sustainable growth rate. It was quite high but began to drop in 1990. As a result of that drop, the stock price has come down, which presents an investment opportunity.

Table 5 is the DuPont analysis for Safety-Kleen. This analysis determines what the company's sources of growth are and what the sources of the increases or decreases in growth are. One of the most important lines is the ratio of sales to total assets. Because of this company's investments during the past few years, its sales–to-total-assets ratio has declined from 1.10 to 0.77. Apparently, the company is becoming less efficient with its asset use, but that trend should reverse as the company brings its new investments on stream and generates more sales, thereby improving its capital efficiency.

To complete the investment decision-making process, we evaluate a large number of companies from our high-quality universe to identify those expected to enjoy above-average sustainable growth during the next five years. Once this set of companies is identified, we use optimization technology to produce an efficient portfolio after setting percentage weightings or constraints to take advantage of those specific sectors in the economy expected to prosper. The risk level of the portfolio is controlled within the optimization process to ensure that we have proper diversification and that our bets about the future do not create inordinate risk for the investor.

Conclusion

The United States has a 70-year history of securities analysis. Significant changes have occurred only twice— during the times of great financial stress in the 1930s and 1970s. The future is largely unknown, but trends now under way and visible suggest another change of great importance, which will probably manifest itself in the application of nonlinear approaches to investing. Static endeavors die. Our profession is dynamic, which ensures its success and vitality, but each practitioner, to remain successful, must also change and adapt. That requires a lifelong commitment to continuing education.

Question and Answer Session

Frederick L. Muller, CFA

Question: In the United States, the validity of active management is being discussed, but Japan might never go through the era of passive management; quantitative active management may be the future course for Japan. Could Japan skip the passive-management phase and go directly to active management?

Muller: Using U.S. history as a guide, if active management in Japan cannot produce results consistent enough to persuade sponsors that incurring the expense of active management is worthwhile, then managers are forced to consider passive management, which is cheaper. The answer is in the marketplace. The buyers of investment management services will make that decision on rational grounds.

Question: In an approach to portfolio composition such as Atlanta Capital's that you described, is there a limit (either upper or lower) to the number of companies included in a universe?

Muller: Our objective is to end up with a portfolio of about 60 stocks. About 800 companies meet our quality criteria, but only about 400 also meet our liquidity criteria. We use the optimizer to reduce the number of companies to a manageable level so we can analyze them in detail. We constrain the optimizer to reflect our expectations of where opportunities lie. For example, we believe small companies offer a better return potential than large ones. We capitalize on this potential by putting a constraint on the optimizer such that the average market capitalization of the companies in the portfolio must be at a certain level.

Question: Can traditional securities analysis be combined with quantitative risk control without diminishing the advantages of either approach?

Muller: One of the reasons we do not use excess returns as an input to the optimizer is that doing so will produce weighting differences that we think go beyond the capability of the model. We essentially equal-weight the securities in the portfolio. We start with a large group of companies screened according to certain criteria, reduce that list of companies to a more manageable number, and do the fundamental or traditional research to satisfy ourselves that the growth rates we expect for the companies are attainable. By the time we move down to the smaller list, all the securities are treated much the same in terms of their return expectations; they are not ranked within the group. When we enter this list of companies into the optimizer, one of the constraints is an equal size requirement for the holdings.

Over a period of about 20 years, equal-weighted portfolios have usually outperformed market-capitalization-weighted portfolios in the United States. That means investors must have an important amount of their assets in what are called small-capitalization companies, which suggests an increase in risk. The optimizer can control the risk while, at the same time, generating a desirable portfolio.

Question: What is the potential of nonlinear models? What is the future of equilibrium models such as the CAPM?

Muller: First, comments about nonlinear models are speculative; little is known about them. The possibility exists that analysts may view investing in quite a different way from the view supported by the CAPM. The profession is faced with limited powers of observation and limited tools for understanding the stock market or other complex phenomena. Thus, nonlinear approaches may offer great powers of observation that will deepen understanding of complex systems. Then, the CAPM will have become a step along the way in the evolution of theory and practice. I do not know whether the CAPM will be displaced any time soon by nonlinear models. I think the CAPM has some problems, and if Kurz's paper is meaningful, the CAPM may be modified or altered to some degree without nonlinear systems being part of the modification.

Question: Please comment on the objectivity of the recommendations of sell-side analysts in the United States.

Muller: Most sell-side firms in the United States have strict rules about not allowing analysts to take advantage of inside information, or any information that might be suggestive of inside information from corporate finance departments. In the late 1960s, McDonnell-Douglas and Merrill Lynch were involved in a famous court case that led to the establishment of a "Chinese wall"—a nonporous wall—between corporate finance and research that is supposed to prevent information from going back and forth between the two.

Some firms have occasionally had a problem with violating the intentions of the Chinese wall, particularly during the 1980s. The investment community at large was damaged because people were not honest.

Top-flight research departments at sell-side firms operate honestly and do not get into a conflict with their corporate clients. When they make a research recommendation about a corporate client, they must disclose that the company is a client of the firm. Sometimes, analysts leave their research departments and go to their corporate finance departments to assist in obtaining underwriting issues. This practice has been particularly visible in the past few years, when the number of equity offerings has been enormous in the United States. This move is not a violation of the law, but some of the best research analysts have shifted to the other side of the Chinese wall, and the quality of research at certain firms may be diminished.

Question: How do you distinguish between a good analyst and a bad analyst?

Muller: Sell-side analysts are basically judged by the marketplace according to how influential their recommendations are with institutions. Each year, *Institutional Investor* surveys the buy-side institutions about who the best analysts are in a particular industry. I suspect the results are significant in the compensation of the sell-side analysts. Some of the investment management companies' analysts on the buy side are outstanding, but outside the organization, one may never hear of them.

Some institutions, whether buy-side or sell-side, will ask how well the recommendations worked in terms of return. Other firms recommend looking at the quality of an analyst's earnings estimates or forecasts; they do not necessarily take into account what happened to the price of the stock, which could be affected by many other factors. Those two attitudes—judging the quality of the business forecast and judging the return on the stock recommended—are probably the two ends of the spectrum. Most judgment criteria are probably somewhere in the middle.

Equity Securities Analysis Case Study: Merck & Company

Bill Kurious, a junior analyst with Grand Concepts Investment Management and a CFA candidate, has been assigned the task of valuing the common stock of Merck & Company. Merck, the world's largest ethical drug manufacturer, discovers, develops, produces, and markets human and animal health products and specialty chemicals. The company has been consistently ranked among the top companies in return on assets and return on sales in *Fortune* magazine's analysis of the 500 largest companies in the United States. It also is considered one of the "most admired" companies in the United States.

Kurious wishes to impress his supervisor, Amy Randall, but is mindful of the high expectations for his performance and the fact that this is his first "real" valuation report. Randall requested that the analysis consider a variety of valuation approaches and that all assumptions be identified explicitly and critically evaluated through sensitivity analysis. Further, Randall directed Kurious to discuss the relative strengths and weaknesses of the valuation methods used in forming his opinion and the associated investment recommendation.

The impending presidential inauguration of Governor Clinton later in the month has greatly complicated Kurious's valuation efforts. The president-elect is known to favor more affordable health care for a broader group of people and advocates a dramatic overhaul of the U.S. health care system. Many analysts believe the new administration will

be tougher on pharmaceutical pricing and that, as a result, the inherent riskiness of the pharmaceutical industry has increased dramatically. Indeed, many investors and analysts believe that the riskiness of the industry cannot be confidently assessed because of the marked political uncertainty surrounding its future.

Notwithstanding these complications, Kurious intends to apply to his assignment the CFA curriculum material on valuation. He decides to pose a series of questions to himself that will guide the valuation process in a methodical fashion. In coming up with these questions, he develops the following notes and observations on Merck, the pharmaceutical industry, and alternative equity valuation methods.

Recent Annual Reports

As of January 1993, Merck had about 38,000 employees and 91,000 stockholders. Sales by non-U.S. subsidiaries were 47 percent of sales in 1989 and 1990 and 46 percent of sales in 1991. The company's most important product names include *Vasotec* and *Prinivil* (inhibitor agents for high blood pressure and angina), *Mevacor* and *Zocor* (cholesterol-lowering agents), *Primaxin* and *Mefoxin* (antibiotics), *Pepcid* (anti-ulcer agent), *Recombivax HB* (hepatitis B vaccine), and *Prilosec* (gastrointestinal). Financial data for Merck are presented in **Appendix A**.

Strategic Objectives

The main thrust of Merck's strategic objectives has been to develop, manufacture, and sell products that reflect progress in science and therapy. Year-to-year objectives include staying

Note: This case was prepared by Randall S. Billingsley, CFA, vice president, Association for Investment Management and Research, and presented by Donald L. Tuttle, CFA, and Gary G. Schlarbaum, CFA

among the leaders in the industry in sales growth, earnings per share, and (cash) return on assets. Operationally, Merck pursues these objectives under the assumption that research and development (R&D) is the key to its long-term growth. Indeed, in 1991, the company spent nearly $1 billion on R&D, which was about 10 percent of all U.S. pharmaceutical R&D spending and about 5 percent of all such spending in the world. According to Merck's 1991 annual report, it planned to increase its R&D spending by about 16 percent in 1992.

Structural Reorganization

Merck realizes that the pharmaceutical industry is becoming increasingly global in research, manufacturing, and marketing. Consistent with that observation, the company decided to reorganize on a global basis in order to increase productivity and to bring into focus its strategic alliances. This reorganization affected its worldwide marketing, vaccines, and manufacturing efforts.

Specifically, Merck created a Human Health Division with the responsibility to market prescription drugs on a global basis. The company's U.S. and international marketing operations were consolidated in this division. The rationale for this shift was that changes in the U.S. health care delivery system are making traditional marketing techniques obsolete. Buyers such as managed health care groups, or health maintenance organizations (HMOs), and hospitals are becoming a growing portion of Merck's customer base. The Vaccine Division was created to seek growth opportunities through internal research and through worldwide strategic alliances. The Manufacturing Division united 31 chemical and pharmaceutical manufacturing plants into a global organization.

Merck's major strategic alliances in 1991 included ventures with AB Astra, DuPont, and Johnson & Johnson. AB Astra/Merck produces *Prilosec* (anti-ulcer) and *Plendil* (hypertension). The DuPont/Merck Pharmaceutical Company produces *Cardolite* (cardiac-imaging agent), *Coumadin* (anticlotting agent), and *IV Persantine* (heart stress testing) and conducts joint research on drugs for Alzheimer's disease. The Johnson & Johnson/Merck Consumer Pharmaceutical Company's primary strategy is to develop over-the-counter versions of certain Merck prescription medicines. One of the first candidates was Merck's *Pepcid*.

Position on Health Care Reform

Merck has observed that the desire to deliver health care to everyone in the United States at costs that society can afford is a major challenge. The annual U.S. health care bill in 1991 was approaching $750 billion, double what it had been seven years earlier. Nevertheless, about 34 million Americans had inadequate or no access to health care in 1991.

Merck argues that pharmaceuticals are the most cost-effective part of the health care system because they often prevent the need for more expensive forms of care. During the past 20 years, the cost of pharmaceuticals as a percentage of the total health care bill has declined consistently.

The company's general position is that everyone should have access to necessary health care services and products. Its stated commitments are to work with public and private organizations to solve problems and to preserve an environment that fosters innovation and risk taking.

Outlook for the Future

Merck is forecasting that competition from generic drugs and from non-U.S. firms will increase. Further, the company expects that health care delivery will continue to shift away from its traditional mode and more toward managed care providers. It believes this trend will slow the escalation of costs in both the private and the government-funded markets. Merck is expecting to acquire new products through licensing, research collaboration, and other strategic alliances. The company is planning to adapt to the economic integration of the European Community market and is encouraging member countries to adopt uniform policies regarding the regulatory review of new products, drug pricing, reimbursement systems, product liability, and patent restoration laws.

Fundamentals of the U.S. Pharmaceutical Industry

After reviewing the particulars of the company itself, Kurious turns his attention to those of the industry in which Merck operates. Data on the major pharmaceutical companies can be found in **Appendix B**.

Pricing and the Demand for Pharmaceuticals

The demand for pharmaceuticals is relatively inelastic. U.S. consumers are not particularly price sensitive because third-party payers (e.g., the government, insurance companies, and large corporate employers) account for the vast majority of health care spending. The implication of demand inelasticity is that the industry is viewed as recession resistant.

The demand for pharmaceuticals is sensitive to significant demographic shifts. The over-65 segment of the U.S. population is increasing. The so-called "greying of America" implies an increase in the demand for pharmaceuticals. Third-party coverage of pharmaceutical costs, however, is neither uniform nor complete throughout the elderly population. Thus, their demand may be somewhat more price elastic than that of the general population.

Consolidation and Joint Ventures

The U.S. pharmaceutical industry has historically been of below-average concentration. It has been composed of numerous medium-sized companies. In recent years, however, the trend toward mergers has reduced the number and increased the size of pharmaceutical companies. Examples of major recent mergers and acquisitions are the merger of SmithKline Beckman with the Beecham Group in a $16 billion deal, the purchase of Squibb by Bristol Myers for $11.5 billion, the purchase of a 60 percent share in Genentech by Hoffman-La Roche for $2.1 billion, the combination of Marion Labs with Merrell Dow, and the acquisition of A.H. Robbins by American Home Products for about $3 billion.

This consolidation trend is expected to slow, replaced by increasing use of joint ventures. Examples include Merck's joint venture with Repligen Corporation to develop an AIDS vaccine, Johnson & Johnson's joint venture with Merck to market over-the-counter products, and Merck's venture with DuPont to develop and market medicines for heart disease and high blood pressure.

Marketing Trends

The Waxman–Hatch Act of 1984 simplified the regulatory approval process for generics. The act has made it easier for firms to bring generic drugs to the marketplace. Major growth is expected in the U.S. generic market because of the Medicare Catastrophic Coverage Act of 1988. Further, patent protection on at least a dozen key drugs will expire in the next few years. The push toward health care reform should increase demand for less expensive generics. Large pharmaceutical companies are moving to gain generic drug production capacity to ease the profit pressure resulting from increased use of generics.

HMOs have been growing and establishing drug utilization programs with broad decision-making ability and large buying power. Further, surveys indicate that patients are changing from passive recipients to active participants in the drug-selection process. Thus, pharmaceutical firms must consider appealing not only to physicians but also to patients.

International Competition

U.S. companies produce about 40 percent of the pharmaceuticals marketed in the world. Although most other countries impose price and/or profit controls that limit the prices of pharmaceuticals, the United States currently has no such controls. For example, pharmaceuticals' prices in European countries in the past 20 years have increased by about half of the general inflation rate. In contrast, the prices of pharmaceuticals in the United States have increased by more than three times the general rate of inflation during the same time period. Such pricing disparities create significant opportunities for non-U.S. firms. The markets for U.S. pharmaceuticals have also been eroded by an alarming increase in the illegal circumvention of U.S. patents and by export restrictions.

The significant dependence of U.S. companies on international sales implies that industry profits are influenced by variations in the value of the U.S. dollar relative to other currencies. A stronger dollar hurts the industry by making U.S. exports less competitive, because non-U.S. products become relatively less expensive.

The U.S. Political/Regulatory Environment

Balancing the concern that the Clinton administration will be tougher on pharmaceutical pricing issues is the possibility that Clinton's emphasis on more comprehensive health care will lead to higher medicine sales volumes. *Value Line* stated that those companies relying more on volume increases than on price increases should prosper under the Clinton administration (*Value Line Investment Survey*, Ratings & Reports, November 6, 1992, p. 1257).

The income earned by U.S. pharmaceutical firms' Puerto Rican operations is currently exempt from U.S. federal income taxes. Some legislators argue that this tax break is at least partially responsible for the alleged excessive profitability in the pharmaceutical industry. President-elect Clinton is known to support a plan that would reduce special tax breaks for the industry.

In April 1992, the Food and Drug Administration (FDA) announced a new program to gain faster access to new drugs and to improve the entire drug review process. The revision in the FDA's procedures is expected to reduce from 10 years to 6 years the average time required to test and win approval for new drugs.

Tasks to Be Completed

Armed with this information about Merck and the industry, Kurious proceeds to organize the report he will present to Randall. Because of the uncertainty surrounding the health care industry, he plans to look at three scenarios—most likely, most pessimistic, and most optimistic—and various growth assumptions. The plan for his analysis includes the following tasks:

1. Briefly describe the current issues involved in marketing pharmaceuticals.

2. Applying Porter's framework for the analysis of competitive strategy, describe the competitive structure of the U.S. pharmaceutical industry. Porter's approach is summarized in the schematic presented in **Exhibit 1**. (For a summary of the Porter framework, see **Appendix C**.)

3. Discuss the extent to which Merck depends on each of the three competitive strategies considered in Porter's model for evaluating the competitive structure of an industry.

4. Evaluate Merck's recent ROE performance using the DuPont ROE decomposition approach presented in **Table 1**. (For a review of the DuPont

Exhibit 1. Competitive Strategy Analysis Framework

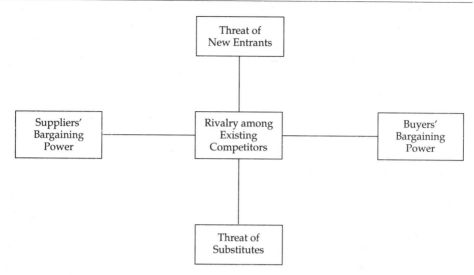

method, see **Appendix D**.) To supplement the ROE analysis, consider the comparative financial ratios provided in the data in **Table 2**.

5. Calculate Merck's intrinsic value using the discounted cash flow (DCF) model by estimating the price that will prevail five years from now (P_5). This application of the DCF model requires that the present value of P_5 be added to the present value of the dividends expected prior to that time.

In calculating the intrinsic value, conduct a sensitivity analysis by assuming that initial dividends, d_0, are $1.00 and the discount rate, k, is 0.1424. Note that the source for the range of growth rates, g_{1-5}, is the analysts' predictions

reported in **Table 3** supplemented with an additional estimate to capture the possibility that the political uncertainty at the time of the case will bring significantly lower growth than analysts are predicting. The estimates for g_{long} reflect potential long-term (i.e., indefinite time horizon) rates beyond the initial five-year period.

Kurious knows that both the single-stage and the multistage versions of the DCF model and the H-model require the analyst to determine the appropriate risk-adjusted discount rate. His readings in the CFA curriculum exposed him to two approaches for determining such rates: the capital asset pricing model (CAPM) and the arbitrage pricing the-

Table 1. ROE Decomposition Analysis: Merck & Company, Year-End 1987–91

Year	ROE	Tax Burden	Interest Burden	Operating Profit Margin	Total Asset Turnover	Leverage
1991	43.16%	67.0%	0.9788	37.61%	0.9057	1.9321
1990	46.45	66.0	0.9748	36.09	0.9554	2.0941
1989	42.47	65.5	0.9772	35.66	0.9695	1.9192
1988	42.26	64.5	0.9607	32.79	0.9693	2.1456
1987	42.82	64.5	0.9614	28.88	0.8911	2.6834
Industry average (1991)	27.6%	71.7%	1.34	13.50%	1.12	1.90

Sources: Calculations are based on the financial statements provided by Merck's 1991 annual report. The industry average is calculated based on the data from "Annual Statement Studies, 1992," by Robert Morris Associates, and *Dow Jones News/Retrieval*.

Table 2. Comparative Financial Ratios: Merck versus U.S. Pharmaceutical Industry, 1987–91

Ratio	1991	1990	1989	1988	1987	Industry Average (1991)
Liquidity						
Current ratio	1.53	1.33	1.78	1.80	1.40	1.70
Acid test	1.18	1.02	1.38	1.43	1.06	1.14
Profitability						
ROA	24.2%	24.1%	23.2%	20.4%	16.8%	13.9%
Leverage						
Interest coverage	18.0×	17.5×	19.3×	17.2×	21.3×	18.7×
Total assets/common equity	1.93	2.09	1.92	2.15	2.68	1.90
Activity						
Asset turnover	0.91	0.96	0.97	0.97	0.89	1.5
Average collection period (days)	64.7	63.2	69.6	62.0	76.6	67.6
Inventory turnover	1.95	1.99	1.99	2.32	2.19	3.8

Sources: Calculations are based on data from Standard & Poor's *Industry Surveys*, RMA's "Annual Statement Studies, 1992," and *Dow Jones News/Retrieval*.

Note: Average yearly data.

ory (APT). Although the validity of the CAPM is a topic of enduring controversy, Kurious believes that it would be relatively straightforward to apply and that it would give him some useful valuation insights. Although he is aware that many analysts and researchers believe the APT approach more accurately and comprehensively reflects investment risk, he believes that it would be more difficult to apply and to explain than the CAPM. Thus, he decided to use the CAPM approach.

Using the following matrix:

g_{1-5}

g_{long}	0.190	0.171	0.140	0.100
0.120				
0.100				
0.080				

a. estimate P_5, and

b. estimate Merck's intrinsic value using the estimated prices from Part a.

6. Using the data in **Table 4, Table**

Table 3. Five-Year Earnings Growth Rate Forecasts: Major Pharmaceutical Companies

Company	Mean	High	Low
Merck	17.1%	19.0%	14.0%
Bristol-Myers Squibb	13.4	19.2	10.0
Marion Merrell Dow	10.4	17.5	3.0
American Home Products	11.6	13.5	10.0
Glaxo	16.5	22.0	11.0

Source: Zacks Investment Research, as reported by *Dow Jones News/ Retrieval*, January 1993.

Table 4. Capital Asset Pricing Model Discount Rate Inputs for Merck

Risk-free rate (30-year U.S. Treasury, 1/11/93)	7.44%
Historical average equity market risk premium $[R_m - R_f]$	6.80%
Beta coefficient (*Value Line*)	1.00
Discount rate $k = R_f + \beta(R_m - R_f)$ $= 0.0744 + 1(0.068)$	14.24%

Sources: The 30-year Treasury rate is from the *Wall Street Journal*, January 1993. The equity market risk premium is from Ibbotson and Sinquefield, *Stocks, Bonds, Bills, and Inflation: Historical Returns (1926–87)*, Charlottesville, Va.: The Research Foundation of the Institute of Chartered Financial Analysts, p. 77.

5, and **Exhibit 2**, apply the two-stage DCF model to estimate the intrinsic value of Merck by relying on *Value Line* and analysts' forecasted growth.

7. Critically evaluate the intrinsic value estimate for Merck produced in Task 6 by performing a sensitivity analysis. Such analysis should illustrate the sensitivity of the valuation to the assumptions made in applying the DCF methodology to Merck. Specifically, show the effects of changes in the underlying determinants of value by completing the following matrix for the most likely, most pessimistic, and most optimistic scenarios:

		k	
	0.1324	0.1424	0.1524
g_s 0.190			
0.171			
0.140			
0.100			

The first three g_s values (see **Appendix E** for an explanation of g_s, "supernormal" growth) correspond to the high, average, and low consensus growth rate forecasts, and the fourth entry reflects the possibility of a significant downward revision in growth expectations as a result of the uncertain political environment. For the most likely scenario,

Table 5. DCF Valuation Model Inputs for Merck: Most Likely Scenario

"Abnormal" growth rate[a]	17.10%
Expected price in 1997[b]	$92.50
Current dividend[c]	$1.00
Current market price (1/11/93)	$43.25

[a] Zacks Investment Research, five-year consensus forecast.
[b] *Value Line*, 1995–97 projections, high = $100, low = $85, average = $92.50. (Assumed value for P_5 = average.)
[c] Most recent annual dividend paid.

assume $P_5 = \$92.50$; for the most pessimistic, assume $P_5 = \$85$; and for the most optimistic, assume $P_5 = \$100$.

8. Discuss the insights derived from the sensitivity analysis performed in Task 7.

9. Use *Value Line*'s predicted price-to-earnings ratio and earnings per share for Merck for 1995 through 1997, as reported in Exhibit 2, to estimate Merck's current intrinsic value. Apply the P/E valuation version of the DCF model as presented in Appendix E. Conduct the analysis under the following assumptions: $d_0 = \$1.00$, $k = 0.1424$, and $g = 0.171$.

10. Discuss the valuation analysis in light of the statistics provided in **Table 6** concerning Merck's price-to-revenue,

Table 6. Recent Price Performance: Merck and U.S. Ethical Drug Industry (as of January 1993)

Item	Merck	Ethical Drug Industry
52-week high	$53.57	$47.74
52-week low	40.50	33.17
5-year high	56.53	44.92
5-year low	15.96	14.38
P/E ratio, last close	20.2	18.7
P/E ratio, 5-year avg. high	24.9	22.7
P/E ratio, 5-year avg. low	15.8	15.3
Price-to-book per share	986%	515%
Price-to-revenue per share	512%	249%

Source: Dow Jones News/Retrieval, January 1993.

Exhibit 2. *Value Line* on Merck, November 6, 1992

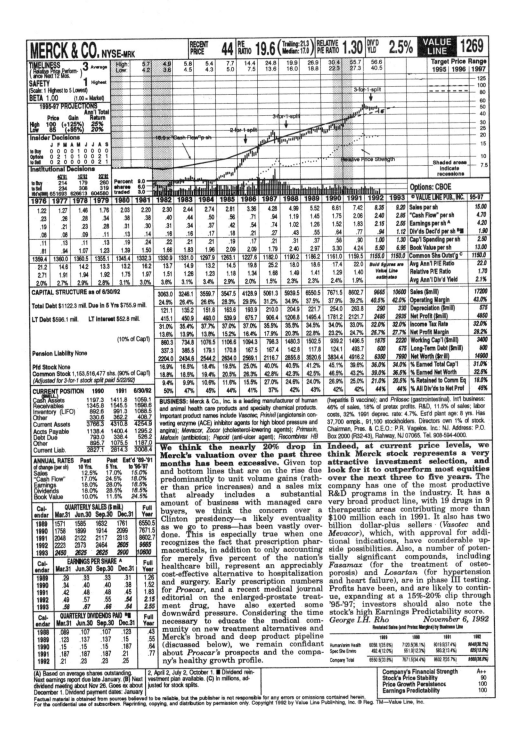

price-to-book-value, and price-to-earnings ratios.

11. Apply the H-model, as presented in Appendix E, to estimate the intrinsic value of Merck. Use the data in **Table 7**.

12. Perform a sensitivity analysis on the H-model results produced in Task 11. Assuming that $d_0 = \$1.00$ and $H = 5$, show the effects of changing the underlying determinants of value by completing the following matrix for each of the three scenarios:

	k		
	0.1324	0.1424	0.1524
g_s 0.120			
0.100			
0.080			

For the most likely scenario, assume g_s = 0.171; for the most optimistic, assume

Table 7. H-Model DCF Inputs for Merck: Most Likely Scenario

"Abnormal" growth rate[a]	17.10%
"Normal" growth rate (g_s)[b]	12.00%
Current dividend (d_n)[c]	$1.00
H estimate[d]	5 years

[a]Zacks Investment Research, five-year consensus forecast.
[b]Possible reversion toward or below current peer average growth rate.
[c]Most recent annual dividend paid.
[d]Ten-year assumed "abnormal" growth period.

g_s = 0.140; and for the most pessimistic, assume g_s = 0.190.

13. Identify the variables that have the greatest effect on the results produced by the H-model.

14. Prepare an overall valuation opinion and investment recommendation for Merck. Be sure to indicate how risk has been taken into account in your analysis.

Appendix A. Merck & Company Financial Data

Table A–1. Consolidated Balance Sheets, December 31, 1989–91
(millions of dollars)

Item	1991	1990	1989
ASSETS			
Current assets			
Cash and cash equivalents	$ 797.7	$ 806.4	$ 685.1
Short-term investments	613.9	390.9	458.4
Accounts receivable	1,545.5	1,345.8	1,265.6
Inventories	991.3	892.6	779.7
Prepaid expenses and taxes	362.2	330.6	221.0
Total current assets	$4,310.8	$3,766.3	$3,409.8
Property, plant, and equipment, at cost			
Land	195.7	169.5	162.1
Buildings	1,483.3	1,258.4	1,129.1
Machinery, equipment and office furnishings	3,002.2	2,660.6	2,417.2
Construction in progress	925.6	542.0	285.5
Total	$5,606.8	$4,630.5	$3,993.9
Less allowance for depreciation	2,102.3	1,908.8	1,701.4
Net property, plant, and equipment	$3,504.5	$2,721.7	$2,292.5
Investments	1,043.7	1,012.3	737.2
Other assets	639.5	529.5	317.2
Total assets	$9,498.5	$8,029.8	$6,756.7
LIABILITIES AND STOCKHOLDERS' EQUITY			
Current liabilities			
Accounts payable and accrued liabilities	$1,400.4	$1,138.4	$ 937.2
Loans payable	338.4	793.0	327.3
Income taxes payable	831.7	679.0	464.8
Dividends payable	243.8	216.7	178.0
Total current liabilities	$2,814.3	$2,827.1	$1,907.3
Long-term debt	493.7	124.1	117.8
Deferred income taxes and noncurrent liabilities	679.7	694.9	701.1
Minority interests	594.6	549.3	509.9
Total liabilities	$4,582.3	$4,195.4	$3,236.1
Stockholders' equity			
Common stock			
Authorized–900,000,000 shares			
Issued–455,524,308 shares	185.7	166.4	152.4
Retained earnings	7,588.7	6,387.3	5,394.2
Total	$7,774.4	$6,553.7	$5,546.6
Less treasury stock, at cost			
68,533,112 shares–1990			
60,116,101 shares–1989	2,858.2	2,719.3	2,026.0
Total stockholders' equity	$4,916.2	$3,834.4	$3,520.6
Total liabilities and equity	$9,489.5	$8,029.8	$6,756.7

Source: Merck annual report, 1991.
Because *Zocor* was only recently approved, there may be a negligible amount of U.S. sales in 1991.

Table A–2. Consolidated Statements of Income, December 31, 1989–91
(millions of dollars, except as noted)

Item	1991	1990	1989
Sales	$8,602.7	$7,671.5	$6,550.5
Costs and expenses			
Materials and production	1,934.9	1,778.1	1,150.3
Marketing and administrative	2,570.3	2,388.0	2,013.4
Research and development	987.8	854.0	750.5
Other (income) expenses, net	(57.0)	(47.4)	(46.7)
Interest income	(162.5)	(152.6)	(147.9)
Interest expense	68.7	69.8	53.2
Exchange losses	51.6	9.6	18.5
Minority interests	25.2	31.5	37.7
Other income, net	(20.0)	(5.7)	(8.0)
Total	$5,436.0	$4,972.7	$4,267.5
Income before taxes	3,166.7	2,698.8	2,283.0
Taxes on income	1,045.0	917.6	787.6
Net income	$2,121.7	$1,781.2	$1,495.4
Earnings per share of common stock ($)	5.49	4.35	3.78

Source: Merck annual report, 1991.

Table A–3. Consolidated Statements of Retained Earnings, December 31, 1989–91
(millions of dollars)

Item	1991	1990	1989
Balance, January 1	$6,387.3	$5,394.2	$4,580.3
Net income	2,121.7	1,781.2	1,495.4
Common stock dividends declared	(920.3)	(788.1)	(681.5)
Balance, December 31	$7,588.7	$6,387.3	$5,394.2

Source: Merck annual report, 1991.

Table A–4. Consolidated Statement of Cash Flows, December 31, 1991

Item	Millions of Dollars
Cash flows from operating activities	
Net income	$2,121.7
Adjustments to reconcile net income to cash provided from operations	
Depreciation and amortization	263.8
Deferred taxes	1.2
Other	(13.0)
Net changes in assets and liabilities	
Accounts receivable	(194.7)
Inventories	(98.7)
Accounts payable and accrued liabilities	226.2
Income taxes payable	157.8
Noncurrent liabilities	(49.5)
Other	19.2
Net cash provided by operating activities	2,434.0
Cash flows from investing activities	
Capital expenditures	(1,041.5)
Purchase of securities, subsidiaries and other investments	(8,800.6)
Proceeds from sale of securities, subsidiaries and other investments	8,518.9
Other	22.6
Net cash used by investing activities	($1,300.6)
Cash flows from financing activities	
Net change in short-term borrowings	(590.6)
Proceeds from issuance of debt	559.8
Payments on debt	(94.1)
Purchase of Treasury stock	(184.1)
Dividends paid to stockholders	(893.2)
Proceeds from exercise of stock options	48.3
Other	15.8
Net cash used by financing activities	($1,138.1)
Effect of exchange rate changes on cash and cash equivalents	(3.8)
Net increase (decrease) in cash and cash equivalents	(8.5)
Cash and cash equivalents at beginning of year	806.4
Cash and cash equivalents at end of year	797.9

Source: Merck annual report, 1991.

Table A–5. Recent Operating Performance: 1992 and 1991
(millions of dollars, except as noted)

Item	1992	1991
Quarter Ending December 31		
Sales	$2,601.1	$2,313.9
Net income	609.1	529.8
Average shares	1,146.8	1,159.5[b]
Net income per share ($)	0.53	0.46[b]
Year		
Sales	9,662.5	8,602.7
Income	2,446.6	2,121.7
Accounting adjustments	(462.4)[a]	
Net income	1,984.2	2,121.7
Average shares	1,153.5	1,159.9[b]
Income per share ($)	2.12	1.83
Net income per share ($)	1.72	1.83[b]

Source: Wall Street Journal, various issues, 1992, 1993.

Notes: Sales of heart drugs *Vasotec* and *Zocor* helped Merck increase sales by 12 percent for the quarter ending 12/31/92. Net income increased 15 percent or 53 cents a share. For 1992, Merck's profit declined 6 percent to $1.98 billion, or to $1.72 a share, on sales of $9.66 billion. Before the effect of three accounting charges, profits rose 17 percent to $2.6 billion, or $2.15 a share.

[a]Cumulative effect of accounting changes.
[b]Adjusted for a three-for-one stock split paid in May 1992.

Table A–6. Selected Financial Data, 1987–91

Year	Earnings per Share	Annual Dividends Paid	Dividend Payout Ratio	Book Value per Share	Return on Equity	Return on Assets
1991[a]	$5.49	$2.31	42.1%	$12.72	48.5%	24.2%
1990	4.56	1.91	41.9	9.90	48.4	24.1
1989	3.78	1.64	43.4	8.91	46.9	23.2
1988	3.05	1.28	42.0	7.20	48.5	20.4
1987	2.23	0.82	36.8	5.37	38.9	16.8

Sources: Value Line, Standard & Poor's *Industry Surveys*, and Merck annual report, 1991.

Note: Based on the average number of shares outstanding during the year.

[a]Three-for-one stock split effective May 1992.

Table A–7. Analysis of Financial Ratios

Ratio	Trend	1991 Relative to Industry
Liquidity		
Current ratio	1988–90 ↓; 1991 ↑	Favorable
Acid test	1988–90 ↓; 1991 ↑	Comparable
Profitability		
ROE	Generally ↑	Superior
ROA	Generally ↑	Superior
Leverage		
Interest coverage	Mixed	Comparable
Total assets/common equity	Mixed	Comparable
Activity		
Asset turnover	Not too variable	Unfavorable
Average collection period	Mixed	Lower/Comparable
Inventory turnover	1987–88 ↑; 1989–91 ↓	Unfavorable

Table A–8. Dividends and Earnings: Merck and the U.S. Ethical Drug Industry, 1987–91

Item	Merck	Ethical Drug Industry
EPS growth	22.5%	14.6%
Dividend growth	30.6	16.7
Average dividend payout	42.0	48.0

Source: *Dow Jones News/Retrieval*, January 1993.

Table A–9. Merck's U.S. Patent Expirations, 1992–2002

Drug	Date of Expiration	1991 U.S. Sales[a] ($millions)
Dolobid	April 1992	$ 35
Timoptic	March 1997	140
Ivermectin	April 1997	257
Noroxin	March 1998	75
Prilosec	March 1998	208
Plendil	April 1998	25
Mefoxin	August 1999	110
Mevacor[a]	November 1999	878
Vasotec[a]	February 2000	745
Pepcid	August 2000	362
Zocor	April 2001	NM
Prinivil	December 2001	154
Primaxin	September 2002	159

Source: FDA, as reported by Morgan Stanley, 1992.

NM = not meaningful.

[a]Morgan Stanley Research estimates. Estimated sales differ significantly from the actual 1991 sales reported in Table B-6.

[b]Because *Zocor* was only recently approved, there may be a negligible amount of U.S. sales in 1991.

Appendix B.   Statistical Data: Pharmaceutical Industry

Table B–1.   U.S. Shipments of Pharmaceutical Preparations, 1989–90
(dollar amounts in millions)

Category	1989 Shipments	Percent of Total	1990[a] Shipments	Percent of Total
Neoplasms, endocrine, metabolic diseases	$ 2,507	8%	$ 2,784	8%
Central nervous system	6,441	20	7,291	21
Cardiovascular system	4,875	15	5,321	15
Respiratory system	3,286	10	3,918	11
Digestive system	4,363	14	4,940	14
Dermatological	1,452	5	1,549	4
Vitamins, etc.	2,672	8	2,663	8
Parasitic, and infective diseases	4,936	16	5,612	16
Veterinary	1,071	3	1,023	3
Total	$31,604	100%	$35,101	100%

Source: Department of Commerce, as reported in "Healthcare: Basic Analysis," Standard & Poor's *Industry Surveys* (August 20, 1992), p. H18.

[a]Latest available.

Table B–2. Product Line Sales and Profits for Major Pharmaceutical Companies, 1991
(millions of dollars)

Company	Product Category	Sales	Profits
American Cyanamid	Medical products	$2,642	$ 383
	Agricultural products	1,206	190
	Chemicals	1,138	32
American Home Products	Health care products	6,220	1,561
	Food products	859	129
Bristol-Myers Squibb	Pharmaceuticals	5,908	1,844
	Medical devices	1,559	354
	Nonprescription health	1,901	435
	Toiletries & household items	1,791	306
Eli Lilly	Life-sciences products	5,726	1,315
Marion Merrell Dow	Pharmaceuticals	2,851	849
Merck	Human/animal health products	8,020	2,996
	Specialty chemicals	583	78
Novo Nordisk	Health care products	1,119	NA
	Bioindustrial products	461	NA
Pfizer	Health care	4,998	814
	Consumer products	696	85
	Agricultural products	526	42
	Specialty chemicals	730	57
Rhone Poulenc Rorer	Pharmaceuticals	3,824	486
Schering-Plough	Ethical pharmaceuticals	2,895	785
	Consumer products	721	156
SmithKline Beecham	Pharmaceuticals	4,619	1,298
	Animal health	595	118
	Consumer products	2,539	434
	Clinical laboratories	1,008	127
Syntex[a]	Pharmaceuticals	1,622	518
	Diagnostics	195	27
Upjohn	Human health care	2,740	715
		662	65
Warner-Lambert	Pharmaceuticals	2,014	488
	Consumer health care	1,960	336
	Confectionery	1,085	134

Source: Company reports, as reported in "Healthcare," Standard & Poor's *Industry Surveys*, p. H18.

NA = not available.

[a]Fiscal year end July 31, 1991.

Table B–3. Foreign Sales by Major U.S. Drug Companies, 1989–91
(dollar amounts in millions)

Company	1989		1990		1991	
	Foreign Sales	Percent of Total Sales	Foreign Sales	Percent of Total Sales	Foreign Sales	Percent of Total Sales
Abbott	$1,838	34%	$2,245	36%	$2,501	36%
American Home Prod.	2,021	30	2,168	32	2,202	31
Bristol-Myers Squibb	3,685	40	4,421	43	4,786	43
Johnson & Johnson	4,876	50	5,810	52	6,199	50
Eli Lilly	2,192	52	2,470	48	2,732	48
Marion Merrell Dow	45	8	675	27	850	30
Merck	3,201	49	3,782	49	4,157	48
Pfizer	2,575	45	2,933	46	3,141	45
Schering-Plough	1,409	45	1,433	43	1,498	41
Syntex[a]	437	32	475	31	561	31
Upjohn	1,096	40	1,200	40	1,290	38
Warner-Lambert	1,947	46	2,242	48	2,444	48

Sources: "Healthcare," Standard & Poor's *Industry Surveys*, p. H22.

Note: Foreign sales are after interarea eliminations, where reported.

[a]Fiscal year end July 31.

Table B–4. Research and Development Expenditures for Major Pharmaceutical Companies, 1989–91
(dollar amounts in millions)

Company	1989		1990		1991	
	R&D Spending	Percent of Sales	R&D Spending	Percent of Sales	R&D Spending	Percent of Sales
Abbott	$502	9%	$567	9%	$666	10%
Bristol-Myers Squibb	789	9	881	9	993	9
Johnson & Johnson	719	7	834	7	980	8
Eli Lilly	605	14	703	14	767	13
Merck	751	11	854	11	988	11
Pfizer	531	9	640	10	757	11
Schering-Plough	327	10	380	11	426	12
SmithKline Beecham	772	9	759	8	808	9
Syntex[a]	245	18	271	18	316	17
Upjohn	407	15	427	14	491	14
Warner-Lambert	309	7	379	8	423	8

Source: "Healthcare," Standard & Poor's *Industry Surveys*, p. H24.

[a]Fiscal year end July 31.

Table B–5. Biggest Gainers in the U.S. Prescription Drug Market, 1991
(dollar amounts in millions)

Product	Manufacturer	Retail Sales 1990	Retail Sales 1991	Percent Change 1990–91
Mevacor	Merck Sharpe & Dohme	$372	$505	36%
Procardia	Pfize	411	510	24
Premarin	Wyeth-Ayerst	236	307	30
Prinivil	Merck Sharpe & Dohme	57	80	41
Zestril	Stuart	72	99	36
Hytrin	Abbott	52	74	42
Axid	Lilly	66	90	36
Ergostat	Parke-Davis	1	2	46
Anafranil	Basel	11	21	93
Duricef	Mead Johnson	63	108	72

Source: Pharmaceutical Data Services, as reported in "Healthcare," *Standard & Poor's Industry Surveys*, p. H26.

Table B–6. Top Prescription Drugs of 1991 Retail Market
(dollar amounts in millions)

Product (Company)	Function	1991 Sales	Percent Change 1988–89
Zantac (Glaxo)	Anti-ulcer	$916	14%
Procardia (Pfizer)	Cardiovascular	510	24
Mevacor (Merck)	Cholesterol reducer	505	36
Cardizem (Marion)	Cardiovascular	475	4
Ceclor (Lilly)	Antibiotic	429	16
Prozac (Lilly)	Anti-depressant	426	5
Vasotec (Merck)	Anti-hypertensive	404	12
Tagamet (SK&F[a])	Anti-ulcer	351	3
Xanax (Upjohn)	Anti-anxiety	338	15
Naprosyn (Syntex)	Anti-arthritic	323	9

Source: Pharmaceutical Data Services, as reported in "Healthcare," *Standard & Poor's Industry Surveys*, p. H26.

Note: Products ranked by total sales.

[a]Smith Kline & French, a subsidiary of SmithKline Beecham.

Appendix C.   Competitive Strategy Analysis Framework

This appendix summarizes the analytical framework presented in Michael E. Porter's influential book, *Competitive Strategy* (New York: The Free Press, 1980).

Forces Determining Industry Competition

I.   Threat of new entrants.
   A.   Barriers to entry.
      1.   Economies of scale. Unit costs decline as absolute volume per period increases.
      2.   Product differentiation. Established firms have brand identification and customer loyalties that differentiate their products from those of the rest of the industry. Differentiation creates a barrier to entry by forcing entrants to spend resources to overcome existing consumer loyalties.
      3.   Capital requirements. Examples include high expense requirements for R&D, production facilities, customer credit, and inventories.
      4.   Switching costs. The high one-time costs when a buyer switches from one supplier's product to another are a barrier to entry. Examples of switching costs include employee retraining costs, the cost of new ancillary equipment, and product redesign costs.
      5.   Access to distribution channels. A new entrant's need to secure distribution channels for its product can be a barrier to entry.
      6.   Cost disadvantages independent of scale. Established firms may have cost advantages that cannot be reproduced by potential entrants regardless of their size and realized economies of scale. Examples include proprietary product technology, favorable access to raw materials, and favorable locations.
      7.   Government policy. Government can limit entry using controls such as licensing requirements and limitations on access to raw materials. Examples of regulated U.S. industries include trucking, railroads, liquor retailing, and freight forwarding. Government restrictions on entry can also come from regulations on elements such as air and water pollution and product safety.
   B.   Expected reaction of existing competition. The threat of entry is influenced by the potential entrant's expectations about the reaction of existing competitors to a new entrant.
II.   Conditions associated with intense rivalry among existing competitors.
   A.   Numerous or equally balanced competitors.
   B.   Slow industry growth.
   C.   High fixed or storage costs.
   D.   Lack of differentiation or switching costs.
   E.   Capacity augmented in large increments (dictated by extent of economies of scale)
   F.   Diverse competitors. Companies that are diverse in strategies, origins, personalities can run into each other in their operations.
   G.   High strategic stakes. Rivalry becomes more volatile as the number of firms with high stakes in achieving success increases.

H. High exit barriers. Examples include specialized assets, fixed costs of exit, strategic interrelationships, and government restrictions.
III. Pressure from substitute products. Substitutes constrain potential returns in an industry by putting a ceiling on prices. The impact of substitutes can be measured by the industry's overall elasticity of demand.
IV. Conditions associated with powerful buyers.
   A. Buyer purchases large volumes relative to seller sales.
   B. Product purchased represents a significant fraction of buyer's costs or purchases.
   C. Product purchased is standard or undifferentiated.
   D. Buyer faces few switching costs.
   E. Buyers earn low profits.
   F. Buyers pose a credible threat of backward integration.
   G. Industry's product is unimportant to the quality of the buyer's products or services.
   H. Buyer has full information.
V. Conditions associated with powerful supplier groups.
   A. Suppliers are dominated by a few companies and are more concentrated than the purchasing industry.
   B. Suppliers need not contend with substitute products for sale to the industry.
   C. Industry is not an important customer of the supplier group.
   D. The suppliers' product is an important input to the buyer's business.
   E. The supplier group's product is differentiated, or there are significant switching costs.
   F. The supplier group poses a credible threat of forward integration.

Generic Competitive Strategies
I. Overall cost leadership strategy.
   A. Description: Cost leadership requires the construction of efficient-scale facilities, the pursuit of cost reductions from experience, tight cost and overhead control, and cost minimization in such areas as R&D, sales, and advertising.
   B. Observations.
      1. A low-cost position can yield above-average returns despite strong competitive forces.
      2. A low-cost position often requires a high relative market share or other advantages.
      3. The strategy can revolutionize an industry in which the nature of competition has been otherwise historically and competitors are unprepared to pursue cost minimization.
II. Differentiation strategy.
   A. Description: Differentiation requires the creation of a product or service that is perceived industrywide as unique.
   B. Approaches to differentiation.
      1. Design or brand image.
      2. Technological superiority.
      3. Superior customer service.
   C. Differentiation and market share. Differentiation may preclude gaining high market share.

III. Focus strategy.
   A. Description: Focusing on a particular buyer group, segments of the product line, or geographic market. The premise of this strategy is that the firm is able to serve its strategic target more effectively or efficiently than competitors that are competing more broadly.
   B. Forms of the focus strategy.
      1. Differentiation within target area.
      2. Cost leadership within target area.

Pursuit of More Than One Generic Strategy

I. It is usually necessary to make a choice among the generic strategies or become "stuck in the middle." The pursuit of more than one strategy is more feasible if the units are strictly separated.
II. Achieving cost leadership and differentiation is usually inconsistent unless:
   A. Competitors are "stuck in the middle."
   B. Cost is strongly affected by share or interrelationships.
   C. A firm pioneers a major innovation.

Sustainability and Above-Average Performance

A generic strategy will not bring above-average performance unless it is sustainable vis-a-vis a firm's competitors. Competitive advantage must resist erosion by competitor behavior or industry evolution.

Appendix D. Review of the DuPont Financial Ratio Analysis Method

The DuPont financial ratio analysis method focuses on explaining how a firm produces its return on equity (ROE) by managing its profit margin, total asset turnover, tax burden, and leverage decisions. **Exhibit D–1** portrays the relationship among these financial ratios, the sustainable growth rate, and a firm's overall balance sheet and income statement.

Exhibit D–1. DuPont Analysis and Sustainable Growth

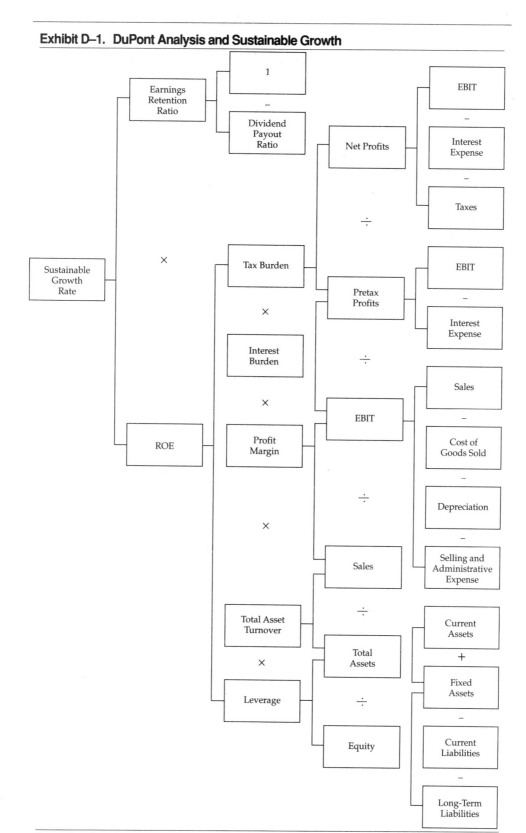

Source: Based on the DuPont model, as presented in Bodie, Kane, and Marcus, *Investments*, 2nd ed. (Homewood, Ill.: Irwin, 1993), pp. 591–94.

Note: EBIT = earnings before interest and taxes.

Appendix E. Selected Valuation Methods

This appendix reviews six widely used methods: the single-stage constant-growth discounted cash flow (DCF) model, the multistage DCF model, the so-called H-model, the price-to-earnings ratio (P/E) approach, the price-to-sales ratio (P/S) approach, and the price-to-book-value (P/B) approach.

Single-Stage Constant-Growth DCF Model

The single-stage constant-growth DCF model values a stock by taking the present value of the cash flows the investment is expected to generate. In practice, this approach implies that an investor or analyst must estimate the company's future earnings per share, project the proportion of earnings that will be paid out as dividends in the future, and calculate the present value of the expected stream of cash flows at the appropriate risk-adjusted discount rate. The single-stage approach assumes that the expected rate of growth will persist indefinitely and that the appropriate discount rate exceeds that growth rate (i.e., growth is "normal"). The basic form of the model is:

$$P_0 = \sum_{t=1}^{\infty} \frac{d_t}{(1+k)^t}$$

$$= \frac{d_1}{(1+k)^1} + \frac{d_2}{(1+k)^2} + \ldots + \frac{d_N}{(1+k)^N}$$

$$= \frac{d_0(1+g)^1}{(1+k)^1} + \frac{d_0(1+g)^2}{(1+k)^2} + \ldots$$

$$+ \frac{d_0(1+g)^N}{(1+k)^N}$$

$$= \sum_{t=1}^{\infty} \frac{d_0(1+g)^t}{(1+k)^t},$$

where P_0 is the current appropriate or intrinsic value of the stock, d_t is the divi-

dend expected in period t, k is the appropriate risk-adjusted discount rate, d_0 is the initial dividend, and g is the expected constant rate of dividend growth.

An equivalent form of the model, restated to facilitate making the necessary calculations, is:

$$P_0 = \frac{d_0(1+g)}{k-g}.$$

This form of the single-stage DCF model is valid only under the assumption that k exceeds g. Further, this and the subsequent forms of the DCF model discussed are not adjusted for the quarterly payment of dividends.

Multistage DCF Model

Many analysts believe it is more realistic to assume that firms pass through various stages of growth that are manifested by different rates of dividend growth. This belief has the analytical convenience of accommodating temporary periods of "supernormal" growth wherein g exceeds k. Consider the two-stage version of the model in which dividends grow at a supernormal rate, g_s $(k < g_s)$, for the first N years and then revert to a normal rate, g_n $(k > g_n)$, indefinitely beyond year N. The valuation impact of g_n is imbedded in the expected price of the stock at the end of year N. Thus, the current price, P_0, is:

$$P_0 = \sum_{t=1}^{N} \frac{d_0(1+g_s)^t}{(1+k)^t} + \frac{P_N}{(1+k)^N}$$

$$= \left[\frac{d_0(1+g_s)}{k-g_s}\right]\left[1-\left(\frac{1+g_s}{1+k}\right)^N\right] + \frac{P_N}{(1+k)^N}.$$

H-Model

The H-model recognizes that an abnormally high growth rate cannot, by definition, be sustained over the long run. Further, it realistically assumes that an abnormal growth rate declines or decays over a period of time rather than shifts immediately from one rate of growth to another, as is implicitly assumed in the two-stage DCF model. Specifically, the H-model values a stock under the assumption that the abnormal growth rate, g_s, decays at a constant rate over a forecasted time frame of $(2 \times H)$ periods. Thus, the growth rate is expected to be one-half of its initial value at time H. The H-model may be stated as:

$$P_0 = \frac{d_0(1+g_n) + d_0(H)(g_s - g_n)}{k - g_n}.$$

Financial Ratios Approaches

Various financial ratios are used as valuation tools. The primary ones are price/earnings, price/sales, and price/book value per share.

Price/Earnings

The ratio of price to earnings per share is viewed as the market's summary opinion of a stock's prospects. As such, it reveals the degree of the market's optimism or pessimism. P/E analysis is a relative rather than an absolute valuation method. It is commonly used to identify stocks that are attractive or unattractive relative to a benchmark (e.g., the overall market's, the industry's, or peer firms' P/Es).

Many analysts use the P/E approach to value common stock directly. The basic approach is to estimate future earnings and the P/E multiple that is expected to be applied by the market at that time in the future. The product of the predicted earnings and the P/E multiple indicates the predicted price of the common stock being valued.

Insight into this approach can be gained by exploring the relationship between the DCF model and the P/E. The single-stage DCF model asserts that

$$P_0 = \frac{d_0(1+g)}{k-g}.$$

Define E_i as expected earnings in period i, b as the earnings retention ratio, and ROE as the return on equity. Thus, the above expression is equivalent to:

$$P_0 = \frac{E_0(1+g)(1-b)}{k-g} = \frac{E_1(1-b)}{k-g} = \frac{E_1(1-b)}{k-(ROE)b}.$$

Therefore:

$$\frac{P_0}{E_1} = \frac{(1-b)}{k-g} = \frac{(1-b)}{k-[ROE]b}.$$

This expression reveals the relationship between P/Es and intrinsic values in the context of the DCF model. This analysis implies that $P_0 = (P_0/E_1)E_1$. The model can be generalized to estimate prices any number of periods in the future. The only constraint on such applications of this approach is the reliability of the forecasted variables.

Price/Sales

The challenges associated with interpreting the reported accounting earnings component present in the P/E have motivated some analysts to use the ratio of price to sales per share (P/S) in valuation. The rationale is that the way most companies report sales is more consistent than the way they report earnings. As is the case for P/E analysis, P/S analysis is a relative valuation approach.

Price/Book Value

The ratio of price to book value per share relates the current market value of a stock to the net worth per share of common stock, as reported on the balance sheet. Book value is thought to reflect the historical value of a firm's assets, net of liabilities, generating the cash flows of the firm. Thus, many analysts assert that book value represents a floor for a stock's price. It is also traditionally used as a relative valuation method.

Guideline Answers: The Merck Case

1. The current issues involved in marketing pharmaceuticals. The major issues in the marketing of pharmaceuticals can be viewed from the perspectives of pricing and of sales volume. The rationale for viewing marketing issues in this manner is that the valuation analysis must address whether Merck's historical growth will continue and where its future growth is likely to come from. The case observes that the demand for pharmaceuticals is relatively price inelastic because most payments are made by third parties. Another observation is that pharmaceutical prices in recent years have increased at roughly three times the U.S. rate of inflation. Thus, the discussion of marketing issues is organized around the question of whether Merck's future growth will come predominantly from price increases or from sales volume increases.

Pricing and volume issues can be evaluated by discussing the implications of four recent developments: the growth of managed health care programs, the aging U.S. population, changes in the role of the consumer/patient, and changes in the U.S. political environment.

■ *Growth of managed health care programs.* Health management organizations are growing in number and are establishing drug utilization programs that have broad decision-making power. Merck's strategic response to this trend was the creation of a Managed Health Care Affairs Department to develop relationships with major HMOs. The widespread presence of such groups could put downward pressure on pharmaceutical prices.

■ *Aging U.S. population.* The so-called "greying of America" implies an increase in the demand for pharmaceuticals. Thus, the aging U.S. population indicates projected growth in sales volume.

■ *Changes in the role of the consumer/patient.* Patients are changing from passive recipients to active participants in the drug-selection process. Merck's strategic response has been to increase its initiatives to involve consumers. An example is the increased use of patient-oriented packaging and advertising. This role change could affect price elasticity adversely from Merck's perspective.

■ *Changes in the U.S. political environment.* In January 1993, the investment community was assessing the implications of President-elect Clinton's stated positions on the pharmaceutical industry. The predominant opinion was that the new administration would be tough on pharmaceutical pricing. The emphasis on more comprehensive, inclusive health care could boost sales volume. Indeed, this policy goal could make the U.S. federal government the largest purchaser of Merck's products in the future. Government product-substitution requirements could greatly increase generic drugs' market share. Greater government involvement could also bring reimbursement policies that include cost-containment goals, which would constrain pharmaceutical prices.

The consensus opinion at this time is that Merck's future growth will most likely come predominantly from growth in sales volume and not from price increases, as was the case in the past.

2. The competitive structure of the U.S. pharmaceutical industry. A schematic analysis of Merck's competitive position, using the Porter approach, is shown in **Exhibit GA–1**.

■ *Buyers' bargaining power.* Buyers' bargaining power is currently low but is expected to grow to a significant level. This growth is expected to result from the consolidation of buyers brought about by the greater prominence of HMOs and greater government

Exhibit GA–1. Merck's Competitive Position in the U.S. Pharmaceutical Industry

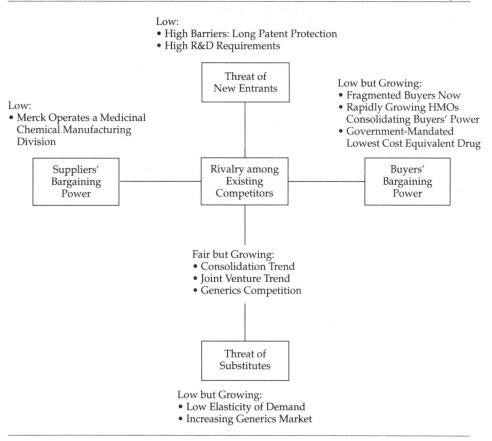

Low:
• High Barriers: Long Patent Protection
• High R&D Requirements

Low:
• Merck Operates a Medicinal
  Chemical Manufacturing
  Division

Low but Growing:
• Fragmented Buyers Now
• Rapidly Growing HMOs
  Consolidating Buyers' Power
• Government-Mandated
  Lowest Cost Equivalent Drug

Threat of
New Entrants

Suppliers'
Bargaining
Power

Rivalry among
Existing
Competitors

Buyers'
Bargaining
Power

Fair but Growing:
• Consolidation Trend
• Joint Venture Trend
• Generics Competition

Threat of
Substitutes

Low but Growing:
• Low Elasticity of Demand
• Increasing Generics Market

participation as a pharmaceutical buyer. Such increased buyer bargaining power would put downward pressure on pharmaceutical prices.

■ *Threat of substitutes.* The price pressure brought by recent government legislation and regulatory change is expected to greatly increase the size of the generic drug market. This eventuality could damage companies that depend heavily on the prescription drug market. Merck is developing over-the-counter drug marketing capabilities such as its joint venture with Johnson & Johnson.

■ *Rivalry among existing competitors.* The increased number of mergers and acquisitions in the pharmaceutical industry could create stronger competitors. Nevertheless, these business combinations and the increasing use of joint

ventures could create a cartel effect that would potentially decrease the degree of competition in the industry.

Joint ventures present interesting possibilities for the industry. Although such ventures spread risk and lower R&D requirements, the larger pharmaceutical firms may be creating stronger competitors by helping smaller firms overcome significant barriers to entry. Alternatively, a joint venture could stunt the growth of a smaller firm's distribution capabilities by making it dependent on the distribution abilities of the larger firm.

3. Porter's model and Merck. Porter identifies three competitive strategies: overall cost leadership, differentiation, and focus.

■ *Overall cost leadership.* Merck

has not pursued this strategy historically because of the pricing flexibility associated with the long patent protection of new drugs.

■ *Differentiation.* Merck in particular and the ethical drug industry in general have highly differentiated products. This differentiation is not exclusively in products but is also in the associated patent protection process and R&D expenditures. Merck is also seeking to differentiate its consumer image, because it views the patient as an increasingly active participant in the drug-selection process. Differentiation is the dominant strategy Merck pursues.

■ *Focus.* Merck has started to focus on HMOs, which are growing in importance as consolidated buying groups. It has conducted a more focused dissemination of information about its products. Focus is a strategy that Merck is increasingly depending upon.

4. Evaluation of Merck's recent ROE performance. Two basic dimensions are considered in ratio analysis: trend analysis, in which the analyst evaluates how a given ratio for a firm has performed *over time*; and comparative or peer analysis, in which the analyst considers how a given ratio for a firm *at a given point in time* compares with the same ratio of peer firms or with a relevant industry average. Rather than interpreting individual ratios in isolation, the ratios should be related to one another to form a representative picture of a firm's overall performance. Ideally, ratio analysis will generate questions that reveal subtle valuation issues.

■ *Trends in ROE performance.* According to Table 1, the trend in Merck's ROE was generally positive during the period from 1987 to 1991. It was never below 42 percent during this period and fell only from 1990 to 1991. Similarly, total asset turnover increased from 1987 to 1989, fell modestly in 1990, and fell significantly in 1991. The tax-burden ratio, defined as the ratio of net profits to pretax profits, increased consistently

during the 1987–91 period. The interest burden rose only modestly during this time period. This result indicates that Merck consistently reduced its tax liability. The operating profit margin improved consistently. Leverage was the most volatile of the DuPont variables. It decreased significantly from 1987 to 1989 and then drifted upward in 1990, only to fall back to its prior level in 1991.

■ *Comparative, or peer, analysis of ROE performance.* Merck compared favorably with the industry averages for ROE and operating profit margin in 1991 (see Table 1). Its leverage was roughly comparable; its interest burden, tax burden, and total asset turnover ratio were all lower than the respective industry averages.

The comparative financial ratios portrayed in Table 2 are largely consistent with the patterns revealed by the DuPont ROE analysis. The lower-than-average total asset turnover ratio in 1991 was accompanied by lower-than-average liquidity as measured by the current ratio. The lower-than-average interest coverage ratio was comparable to the industry's, as was the leverage ratio. Merck's average collection period was shorter than the industry average in 1991.

■ *Overall interpretation of the ratio analysis.* The primary source of Merck's exemplary ROE performance was its ability to increase steadily the already dramatic levels of its operating profit margin from 1987 to 1991. Merck's accomplishment reflects its product mix. Merck is more a pure ethical drug company than most of the other firms in the industry. Ethical drugs have a higher margin than other products. For example, some of the companies in the industry have consumer product businesses that have thin margins. Other companies sell medical supplies, which also tend to have lower margins, as part of their product mixes. Thus, comparisons between Merck's lofty operating profit margins and the industry average must be made cautiously because of the differences between Merck's product mix and those of other firms.

Caution must also be exercised in interpreting the significance of the decline and lower level of Merck's total asset turnover ratio. When turnover ratios fall, a firm is typically perceived to be having a problem maintaining efficiency. For example, a marked decline or low comparative level in inventory turnover is generally interpreted as negative. Total asset turnover is not so easily interpreted, however. This ratio can fall because a firm is investing heavily in assets to enhance its future efficiency. Thus, in the short run, asset turnover and ROE can suffer but will actually benefit from such investment over the long term.

The potential implications of Merck's enviably high ROE are important in light of the extremely uncertain political environment facing the U.S. pharmaceutical industry in 1993. Since 1988, Merck's ROE has never been lower than 42 percent. Such a high return could be viewed as a tempting target for regulators, who might wonder why any firm would need such high earnings. The uncertain political environment also has potential implications for Merck's ability to continue increasing its operating profit margin.

The company's expected future growth is presumably heavily reliant on increasing profit margins, the primary source of its growth in the recent past. Yet, in 1993, the press was publishing stories about high pharmaceutical prices and the need for cost containment. Thus, Merck's ability to depend on aggressive product pricing and, by implication, high margins to enhance its future growth is in question.

5. Calculate Merck's intrinsic value. The technique for estimating intrinsic value that is indicated by the form of the data is:

$$P_0 = \sum_{t=1}^{5} \frac{d_0\,(1+g_{1-5})^t}{(1+k)^t} + \frac{P_5}{(1+k)^5}$$

$$= \frac{d_0(1+g_{1-5})}{k-g_{1-5}} + \left[1 - \left(\frac{1+g_{1-5}}{(1+k)}\right)^5\right]$$

$$+ \frac{P_5}{(1+k)^5}.$$

This technique requires an estimate of P_5, which can be done using the following formula:

$$P_5 = \frac{d_6}{k-g} = \frac{[d_0(1+g_{1-5})^5](1+g_{long})}{(k-g_{long})}$$

The expected P_5 values under the DCF model sensitivity analysis are as follows:

		g_{1-5}			
		0.190	0.171	0.140	0.100
g_{long}	0.120	$119.32	$110.09	$96.27	$80.52
	0.100	$61.91	$57.12	$49.95	$41.78
	0.080	$41.30	$38.11	$33.32	$27.87

Using these estimated prices, the intrinsic value sensitivity analysis for Merck is as follows:

		g_{1-5}			
		0.190	0.171	0.140	0.100
g_{long}	0.120	$66.98	$61.97	$54.45	$45.85
	0.100	$37.48	$34.74	$30.64	$25.94
	0.080	$26.89	$24.97	$22.09	$18.79

6. Calculate Merck's intrinsic value using a two-stage DCF model. The two-stage discounted cash flow model for Merck is calculated as follows for the most likely scenario:

$$P_0 = \sum_{t=1}^{5} \frac{d_0\,(1+g)^t}{(1+k)^t} + \frac{P_5}{(1+k)^5}$$

$$= \sum_{t=1}^{5} \frac{1.00(1.171)^t}{(1.1424)^t} + \frac{92.50}{(1.1424)^5}$$

$$= \$52.92$$

Exhibit GA–2 presents the risk/return implications of the above valuation using a simplified application of the capital asset pricing model. Merck is viewed as undervalued because the prevailing market price of $43.25 was below its appropriate price, or intrinsic value, of $52.92. Merck was also undervalued from a rate of return perspective, because the expected return, $E(k)$, implied by the purchase of the stock at its market price was 19.16 percent, which exceeds the appropriate expected return of 14.24 percent predicted by the capital asset pricing model. The expected return of 19.16 percent is calculated by solving the following equation for $E(k)$:

$$\$43.25 = \sum_{t=1}^{5} \frac{1.00(1.171)^t}{[1+E(k)]^t} + \frac{92.50}{[1+E(k)]^5}$$

7. Intrinsic value sensitivity analysis.

The matrix of intrinsic values for each of the three scenarios is shown below:

Most Likely Scenario
$P_5 = \$92.50$

		k	
	0.1324	0.1424	0.1524
0.190	$55.49	$53.20	$51.02
0.171	$55.21	$52.93	$50.76
∞ 0.140	$54.78	$52.51	$50.35
0.100	$54.26	$52.01	$49.87

Most Pessimistic Scenario
$P_5 = \$85.00$

		k	
	0.1324	0.1424	0.1524
0.190	$51.46	$49.35	$47.33
0.171	$51.18	$49.07	$47.07
∞ 0.140	$50.75	$48.65	$46.66
0.100	$50.23	$48.15	$46.18

Most Optimistic Scenario
$P_5 = \$100.00$

		k	
	0.1324	0.1424	0.1524
0.190	$59.52	$57.05	$54.71
0.171	$59.24	$56.78	$54.45
∞ 0.140	$58.80	$56.36	$54.04
0.100	$58.29	$55.86	$53.56

The values of the growth rate correspond to the high, average, and low consensus growth rate forecasts. The fourth line reflects the possibility of a significant downward revision in growth expectations as a result of the uncertain political environment at the time this case was written.

8. Discussion of intrinsic value sensitivity analysis.

Under all three scenarios, which include various assumptions for the growth rate, the appropriate required rate of return, and the expected price in five years, the intrinsic value of Merck is in excess of its market price of $43.25.

The results produced by the DCF model are influenced heavily by *Value Line*'s predicted future price for Merck. Although the five-year consensus growth rate forecasts are important, they are much less important than the anticipated price. One way of envisioning this point is to consider the growth rate expected beyond the next five years that is implied by the price expected in five years (P_5). The implied long-term growth rates under the three future price scenarios and an assumed required rate of return of 14.24 percent are calculated as follows:

$$P_5 = \frac{d_6}{(k-g)}.$$

Therefore, the implied g_{long} equals

$$[d_0(1+g_{1-5})^5/P_5] - k.$$

The implied long-term growth rates are as follows (solving for the implied growth rates is an iterative process, so

Exhibit GA–2. Risk/Return Implications of Merck Valuation: Two-Stage Discounted Cash Flow Model

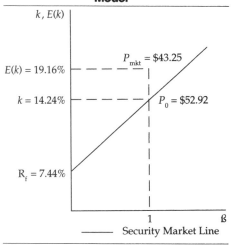

$k, E(k)$

$E(k) = 19.16\%$

$P_{mkt} = \$43.25$

$k = 14.24\%$

$P_0 = \$52.92$

$R_f = 7.44\%$

1

ß

——— Security Market Line

Notes:

k = Appropriate or required rate of return given Merck's recent β of 1.

$E(k)$ = Expected rate of return on Merck given its current market price.

P_{mkt} = Merck's January 11, 1993, market price.

P_0 = Merck's appropriate or intrinsic value.

R_t = Current risk-free rate, which is the yield on long-term (30-year) U.S. T-bonds as of January 11, 1993.

some rounding errors should be expected):

P_5

	\$85.00	\$92.50	\$100.00
0.190	11.12%	11.37%	11.58%
0.171	11.36%	11.58%	11.78%
0.140	11.71%	11.91%	12.08%
0.100	12.12%	12.29%	12.43%

g^{1-5}

The expected future prices range from \$85 to \$100. The narrowness of this range does not allow significant variation in the implied future (i.e., long-term or indefinite) growth rates for the given range of five-year expected growth rates. The implied growth rates range from only 11.12 percent to 12.43 percent, which is consistent with the range in intrinsic values from \$48.15 to \$57.05.

9. Calculation of intrinsic value using Merck's P/E and EPS. Exhibit 2 shows that as of November 6, 1992, *Value Line* was forecasting an EPS of \$4.20 and an average P/E of 22.0 in the 1995–97 period. Given that $(P_0/E_1)E_1 = P_0$, then $(P_{96}/E_{97})E_{97} = P_{96}$, and the predicted price for Merck in 1996 is \$92.40 (22 × \$4.20). This is consistent with Merck's explicit projections for its price during 1995 to 1997: a high of \$100 and a low of \$85. The average of the high and low projections is \$92.50, which is equal to the projection for the price in 1996 indicated by the P/E approach using *Value Line's* data.

Intrinsic value is estimated by adding the present value of the projected price in 1996 to the present value of the dividends received up to that point in time. Assume for simplicity that this is four full years. Thus, under the indicated assumptions:

$$P_0 = \sum_{t=1}^{4} \frac{d_0(1+g)^t}{(1+k)^t} + \frac{P_{96}}{(1+k)^4}$$

$$= \frac{d_0(1+g)}{k-g}\left[1-\left(\frac{1+g}{1+k}\right)^N\right] + \frac{P_{96}}{(1+k)^4}$$

$$= \frac{1.00(1.171)}{0.1424-0.171}\left[1-\left(\frac{1.171}{1.1424}\right)^4\right]$$

$$+ \frac{92.40}{(1.1424)^4} = \$58.51.$$

10. Discussion of the valuation analysis. Table 6 shows that Merck's price-to-revenue ratio (P/R) is about 2.06 times greater than the industry average, its P/B is about 1.91 times greater than the industry average, and its P/E is only 1.08 times greater than the industry average. Apparently, investors are paying more for asset-based sources of growth, as measured by the P/R and P/B, than for Merck's earnings, as measured by its P/E. The P/E analysis performed for the preceding task provides no insights beyond those yielded by the DCF model analyses.

11. Calculation of intrinsic value using the H-model. The following H-model valuation shows that the intrinsic value of Merck is $61.38. Note that the long-term growth rate is assumed to be 12 percent under the rationale that Merck's expected long-term growth rate could fall because of the implications of the uncertain political environment:

$$P_0 = \frac{d_0(1 + g_n) + d_0(H)(g_s - g_n)}{(k - g_n)}$$

$$= \frac{1.00(1.1200) + 1.00(5)(0.1710 - 0.1200)}{0.1424 - 0.1200}$$

$$= \$61.38.$$

12. Sensitivity analysis of the H-model.
The effects of changing the underlying determinants of value are as follows:

Most Likely Scenario
$g_s = 17.10\%$

		k		
		0.1324	0.1424	0.1524
g_n	0.12	$110.89	$61.38	$42.44
	0.10	$ 44.91	$34.32	$27.77
	0.08	$ 29.29	$24.60	$21.20

Most Pessimistic Scenario
$g_s = 14.00\%$

		k		
		0.1324	0.1424	0.1524
g_n	0.12	$98.39	$54.46	$37.65
	0.10	$40.12	$30.66	$24.81
	0.08	$26.34	$22.12	$19.06

Most Optimistic Scenario
$g_s = 19.00\%$

		k		
		0.1324	0.1424	0.1524
g_n	0.12	$118.55	$65.63	$45.37
	0.10	$ 47.84	$36.56	$29.58
	0.08	$ 31.11	$26.12	$22.51

13. Analysis of the H-model results.
Careful evaluation of the sensitivity analysis of the H-model indicates that the difference between k and g_n has the greatest effect on pricing in this model. Further, the results are more sensitive to the forecasted g_n than to the shorter term forecasted g_s.

14. Overall valuation opinion and investment recommendation.
A plausible argument can be made for either a buy or a sell recommendation based on the relative importance placed on the various pieces of evidence. Ultimately, the valuation opinion depends heavily on whether Kurious believes that Merck can sustain its impressive operating profit margin, earnings growth, and ROE.

Although valuation always involves forecasting and judgment, the especially uncertain political and regulatory environments at the time of this valuation make Merck enormously difficult to value. An analysis of Merck should include both quantitative and qualitative factors.

Observations on Quantitative Factors

The following points relate to the quantitative aspects of the analysis:

▓ *DuPont ROE analysis.* Merck's admirable ROE levels have been driven in recent years largely by the high levels and rate of growth in its operating profit margin. Analysis of the P/Rs, P/Bs, and P/Es suggests that Merck's market price is affected more by asset-based factors than by earnings-based factors. Interestingly, however, consensus five-year forecasted earnings growth rates were in the range of 14 to 17 percent at this time. Similarly, *Value Line* was predicting that Merck's price would be between $85 and $100 in the period from 1995 to 1997. Valuation models can provide insight into the implications of such high forecasted growth rates and future prices.

▓ *Valuation model results.* The initial DCF model sensitivity analysis, which focuses on the expected price of Merck in five years (P_5), produced intrinsic values in excess of Merck's current price for all expected short-term growth rates (g_{1-5}) only under the assumption that the long-term growth rate (g_{long}) was 0.12 or higher. Under g_{long} assumptions of 0.10 and 0.08, Merck was overvalued for all assumed values of g_{1-5}. The two-stage DCF model under various assumptions produced intrinsic values that were all in excess of Merck's prevailing market price of $43.25. The H-model under various assumptions produced more mixed results than the two-stage DCF model.

Depending on which normal growth rate, abnormal growth rate, and discount rate Kurious has the most confidence in, Merck could be viewed as either over- or undervalued. Although the evidence provided by the two-stage DCF model generally indicated that Merck is undervalued, the evidence provided by the initial DCF model and H-model was mixed and generally less supportive of that valuation opinion.

▨ *Pitfalls in quantitative analysis.* The quantitative analysis of Merck is only as good as the assumptions made concerning the underlying determinants of value. The primary way to take risk into account in quantitative analysis is through the assumed discount rate. Thus, Kurious must judge the reasonableness of the forecasted growth rates and the discount rate used in his analysis. The discount rates assumed in this case can be criticized on the grounds that they were estimated using only a simplified application of the CAPM. Even if that model is accepted as the best approach, analysts differ in their approaches to estimating the required parameters. For instance, some would take issue with the chosen proxy for the risk-free rate and with the value of the risk premium, especially in light of the observation that risk premiums widen during periods of lower interest rates. Further, one might argue that another approach, such as the APT, might be a more useful way to estimate the discount rate.

Observations on Qualitative Factors

The valuation of Merck dramatically illustrates the potential dangers of extrapolating from historical data. Merck has been one of the most admired companies in the world and has produced dramatic investment results. An analyst, however, must always ask how applicable the past is to the future. This question can only be answered by determining how Merck generated its growth in the past and by evaluating how sustainable that growth will be in the future.

As noted above, the primary source of Merck's growth in the recent past was its operating profit margin. In light of the significant uncertainty concerning the implications of the new administration's evolving health care policy reforms, Merck appears unlikely to sustain its growth by relying on significant pharmaceutical price increases. Thus, Merck's future growth appears to be more dependent on volume increases. Merck's historical product-mix strategy could dampen such growth somewhat. Further, potential adverse legislative developments such as the removal of the Puerto Rican tax shelter for U.S. pharmaceutical companies could also restrain Merck's growth by increasing its future tax liability. A convincing argument can therefore be made that Merck will not be able to sustain its dramatic growth record in the future. Depending on how much Kurious believes that future growth will decline, Merck could be viewed as either over- or undervalued.

Order Form₀₂₅

Additional copies of *Equity Securities Analysis and Evaluation* (and other AIMR publications listed on page 97) are available for purchase. The price is **$20 each in U.S. dollars**. Simply complete this form and return it via mail or fax to:

AIMR
Publications Sales Department
P.O. Box 7947
Charlottesville, Va. 22906 U.S.A.
Telephone: 804/980-3647
Fax: 804/977-0350

Name _____

Company _____

Address_____

_____ Suite/Floor _____

City _____

State_____ ZIP_____ Country_____

Daytime Telephone_____

Title of Publication	**Price**	**Qty.**	**Total**
_____	____	____	____
_____	____	____	____

Shipping/Handling
- ❏ All U.S. orders: Included in price of book
- ❏ Airmail, Canada and Mexico: $5 per book
- ❏ Surface mail, Canada and Mexico: $3 per book
- ❏ Airmail, all other countries: $8 per book
- ❏ Surface mail, all other countries: $6 per book

Discounts
- ❏ Students, professors, university libraries: 25%
- ❏ CFA candidates (ID #_____): 25%
- ❏ Retired members (ID #_____): 25%
- ❏ Volume orders (50+ books of same title): 40%

Discount $_____

4.5% sales tax
(Virginia residents) $_____

8.25% sales tax
(New York residents) $_____

7% GST
(Canada residents,
#124134602) $_____

Shipping/handling $_____

Total cost of order $_____

❏ Check or money order enclosed payable to **AIMR**   ❏ Bill me
Charge to: ❏ VISA   ❏ MASTERCARD   ❏ AMERICAN EXPRESS

Card Number:_____ ❏ Corporate ❏ Personal

Signature:_____   Expiration date: _____

Selected AIMR Publications*

The CAPM Controversy: Policy and Strategy Implications for Investment Management, 1993 . . . . $20
Diana R. Harrington and Robert A. Korajczyk, *Editors*

The Health Care Industry, 1993 . . . . $20
James Balog, *Editor*

Predictable Time-Varying Components of International Asset Returns, 1993 . . . . $20
Bruno Solnik

The Oil and Gas Industries, 1993 . . . . $20
Thomas A. Petrie, CFA, *Editor*

Execution Techniques, True Trading Costs, and the Microstructure of Markets, 1993 . . . . $20
Katrina F. Sherrerd, CFA, *Editor*

Investment Counsel for Private Clients, 1993 . . . . $20
John W. Peavy III, CFA, *Editor*

Active Currency Management, 1993 . . . . $20
Murali Ramaswami

The Retail Industry—General Merchandisers and Discounters, Specialty Merchandisers, Apparel Specialty, and Food/Drug Retailers, 1993 . . . . $20
Charles A. Ingene, *Editor*

Equity Trading Costs, 1993 . . . . $20
Hans R. Stoll

Options and Futures: A Tutorial, 1992 . . . . $20
Roger G. Clarke

Improving the Investment Decision Process—Better Use of Economic Inputs in Securities Analysis and Portfolio Management, 1992 . . . . $20
H. Kent Baker, CFA, *Editor*

Ethics, Fairness, Efficiency, and Financial Markets, 1992 . . . $20
Hersh Shefrin and Meir Statman

Investing Worldwide, 1992, 1991, 1990 . . . . $20 each

The Financial Services Industry—Banks, Thrifts, Insurance Companies, and Securities Firms, 1992 . . . . $20
Alfred C. Morley, CFA, *Editor*

Managing Asset/Liability Portfolios, 1992 . . . . $20
Eliot P. Williams, CFA, *Editor*

Investing for the Long Term, 1992 . . . . $20

*A full catalog of publications is available from AIMR, P.O. Box 7947, Charlottesville, Va. 22906; 804/980-3647; fax 804/977-0350.